This Golden Round

This Golden Round

THE ROYAL SHAKESPEARE COMPANY AT THE SWAN

RONNIE MULRYNE
MARGARET SHEWRING

Mulryne and Shewring Ltd.
in association with
A. H. Jolly (Editorial) Ltd.

Sponsored by Jaguar Cars Ltd.

For Eithne and John

Published by Mulryne and Shewring Ltd,
30 Avenue Road, Stratford-on-Avon, CV37 6UN
in association with A. H. JOLLY (EDITORIAL) LTD.

© Copyright Mulryne and Shewring Ltd.
First Printing 1989

ISBN 0 948308 06 X PAPERBACK
       0 948308 07 9 CASEBOUND

Designed and produced by
A. H. JOLLY (EDITORIAL) LTD
YELVERTOFT MANOR, NORTHAMPTONSHIRE, NN6 7LF.

Printed in Great Britain by
JOLLY & BARBER LTD, RUGBY, WARWICKSHIRE

Contents

Preface

My last years at the helm of the Royal Shakespeare Company were dominated by the problems and pleasures of building and opening the Swan Theatre, and I am unashamedly proud when I return to Stratford these days and see on the skyline the only tangible evidence that I worked there for more than twenty years. It is of course entirely right that people move on, principles are modified, regimes find new goals and that the achievements of the past live where theatrical success and failure always and exclusively live, in the individual memory. But even so, it is immensely satisfying to know that a building stands and operates where otherwise it would not. The sonnets will indeed long outlast both marble and gilded monuments just as they outlasted the Globe playhouse, but a playhouse in turn has a relatively permanent value both because of and in spite of the succeeding generations who use it.

The Swan is an act of defiance. Throughout the land in recent years theatres have been closing. The surge of new building funded by the Arts Council and Local Authorities which produced the various delights of the Nottingham Playhouse, the Sheffield Crucible, the Leicester Haymarket and many more is long past, and just when it seemed that as many as five percent of our population might visit a theatre in a year, a penny-pinching treasury parsimony has crippled the Arts Council and brought about an alarming erosion of both fringe and regional theatre.

The RSC was given terse warnings by both Arts Council and Arts Ministry officials that could have been interpreted as proscription and interdiction – ye shall not build, ye shall not expand, and if ye do, ye are on your own – but we chose, like Nelson, to read them with our blind eye.

When finally the new theatre opened in 1986, thanks to the legendary generosity of Mr Frederick Koch, it was unanimously welcomed as a beautiful, stimulating, communal performing space and as the home of a unique and much-lacked repertoire which would help critics and public alike to appreciate more of this country's dramatic heritage than ever before. Perhaps when I retired as Artistic Director after the opening of the Swan, the public and private silence from both Arts Council and Arts Ministry that greeted my departure was because I did not sufficiently apologise.

The Swan is not the first and we must all pray, not the last national treasure to come into being against the wishes of officialdom. But it is in a much more important sense characterised by defiance. By the end of the century, the long predicted deluge of home screen channels and facilities will have arrived and the advertising man will have come to dominate all areas of our cultural life, from the selection of governments to the complexion of education, to the professionalising of all sport, to the rejection of everything that is dramatically complex or difficult in narrative entertainment. The BBC is clearly doomed from the moment when the licence fee system is curtailed, which will almost certainly precede the expiry of its royal charter. Programming formulae will be defined by what sells and these criteria will be established by advertising men with competition to beat. The much vaunted expansion of 'choice' will in reality be a huge increase in availability of a much smaller range of expression.

In this superficially jolly not too distant future, subsidised theatres will be viewed with increasing ruthlessness as lame ducks. Market forces cannot distinguish between a packed out summer theatre season of 'Allo 'Allo and a poorly attended Timon of Athens: the receipts would be proof positive that the Shakespeare has no viability. Fewer repertory theatres do Shakespeare these days; the costs are too high; a musical has a more certain return. If the trend continues, accompanied by a concomitant downgrading of classical training for young actors, the performance of Elizabethan plays could quite quickly become a museum-like activity not dissimilar from the presentation in aspic of Japan's Noh theatre.

But the Swan is dedicated to exploring our past, assessing our influences, living through our heritage and preserving humility and sanity in a mercantile world in which all history is predictably bunk.

It is worth reminding ourselves that in Huxley's piercingly prescient Brave New World, the savage, captured from the pre-revolutionary ancient wilderness, can communicate only in half-remembered snatches of Shakespeare's verse. Now is the time for defiance.

London,
January 1989

Trevor Nunn.

garden impression

MICHAEL REARDON & ASSOCIATES, Chartered Architects

Introduction

From its opening in the spring of 1986, the Swan Theatre at Stratford-upon-Avon has been greeted by press and public as a visually appealing and theatrically exciting space. *The Observer* commented on 'Michael Reardon's pale golden galleried playhouse' and wrote in glowing terms about its 'precision, harmony, versatility, joy'. *Punch* thought the Swan 'the most exciting dramatic space' to have opened during its critic's playgoing lifetime. As the begetter of the enterprise, Trevor Nunn described how the ugly duckling of the old Rehearsal Room, now 'beautiful, elegant and fulfilled', had been transformed into a beguiling Swan. Even those who found the auditorium's style not their style – there were some for whom the varnished new wood of stage and galleries brought Conran to mind or Habitat – conceded that the theatre *had* style, and a certain vivacity, order and clarity. No one, at least, disputed the excellence of its acoustics. Michael Reardon, the architect, spoke of 'tuning' the theatre space. Some compared the auditorium to the tense bracing of a stringed instrument, violin or at lowest viola in pitch. One or two criticisms were voiced. A few theatre-goers found the seating less than perfect, with sight-line problems in the stalls, and a number of seats on the upper levels partially blocked, or requiring their occupants to perch like birds on a bough. Directors and actors found themselves coping with a lack of wing space and tortuous exits and entrances. Yet whatever the criticisms, by universal consent Trevor Nunn and Michael Reardon, with their colleagues, had brought into being a supremely distinctive theatre space, conjured out of nothing – or almost nothing – by the magic of theatrical and architectural imagination. The event was one to celebrate in the rather mixed annals of theatre-building in Britain in the modern period.

Since the first enthusiastic response – so intense, one of our contributors claims, that during the first season critics reviewed the auditorium and not the plays – the Swan has continued to provoke lively reactions. Now that the repertoire has extended to three seasons, audiences and theatre personnel have come to acknowledge not only the building's flair, but its strong personality as a performance space. As the timbers have gradually settled and twisted, and the wood has mellowed in colour and here and there split, the vivid presence of the galleried theatre has continued to make itself felt as an active agent in performance. When working at the Swan, directors, actors and designers have each been conscious of taking on a strongly-characterised space. Audiences have been aware, before and during the shows, not only of each others' faces across the stage, but of the shadowy yet insistent presence of the rails and ranked galleries that make up the auditorium – a tonal influence on their experience, and more broadly perhaps an aesthetic and even social one. The unusually-elongated promontory stage has asserted its presence for performers and audiences alike: a tongue that juts out into the midst of the theatre space, the stage has assumed the character of a public platform and a place for display, rather than a place for introspection and soliloquy. These features have both stimulated theatre-people and made them wary. Designers especially have found the space a challenge. The soaring height of the theatre, in relation to its width, has given certain actors and directors, as well as designers, new inspiration; to others it has seemed technically resistant. A number of productions have appeared very much at home, others have had to find their style in opposition to the building's particular qualities. All have had to negotiate with the Swan's vivid individuality.

It is unusual perhaps to devote a book to a contemporary theatre and its repertoire, rather than, say, to a dramatist or a dramatic genre, to a company of players or a theatrical era. Yet the interaction between script and space is one of the essentials of theatre. Each space has its own distinct character, the product of its dimensions, its architectural features, its ordering of the relationship between audience and stage, and even, as contributors to this book suggest, its social and physical environment. This distinct character opens up opportunities for actor, director, designer and musician; it also limits choices and affects style. It seemed to us that the work of the Swan during its first three seasons provided an unusual opportunity to study the interaction between a relatively homogeneous yet varied group of scripts, and a theatre as characterful as any in modern Britain. The decision to employ the Swan for the performance of infrequently revived seventeenth-century plays gave its repertoire the character of an experiment, however incompletely or even timidly that experiment may have been carried out. We have thought it worthwhile to report the results of the experiment, conditioned as they were by taking place in that particular theatre. We have confined ourselves to the work of the

Royal Shakespeare Company during the seasons in question, leaving out of account the visiting companies who also worked in the Swan, in order to observe the main work more closely, and to provide some kind of focus.

We do not intend this as a reference book, although we have provided cast lists for all the productions, and we have included in our chapter on the repertoire a brief discussion of each show. Nor is it our aim to be comprehensive, or to devote equal attention to all the productions. Rather, we wish to provide perspectives on the life of the Swan, including the experience of working in it as a theatre professional, as well as the experience of attending the shows. We begin with the building itself, however, as the setting for the shows and, as explained above, a conditioning element in each production. Michael Reardon's piece describes the history of the project, as seen by the architect, and sets out some of the theatre's architectural features. Trevor Nunn gives in his Preface a political context for the development of the Swan; his second piece narrates the development of the theatre project and its objectives. Terry Hands looks towards a Future for the Swan. James Sargant took responsibility for much of the practical administration involved in getting the theatre into commission; he provides an account of the Swan as a workplace for a wide variety of skills. The day-to-day business of managing the theatre has fallen largely to Geoff Locker, who outlines the practical abilities necessary to its efficient operation. The bulk of the book is given over, however, to edited interviews with directors, designers and actors, together with a music director and composer, and a voice director. We hope in this way to evoke as freshly and vividly as possible the experience of working in the Swan, and the nature of the shows which have been presented there; each theatre professional comments both on his or her personal response to the auditorium and on the shows they have helped to realise. We have resisted the temptation to rewrite these interviews into a standard form of English, preferring to retain the directness of a more colloquial idiom. Our other contributions, by contrast, offer considered responses to some part of the Swan repertoire. Michael Billington writes as a national theatre critic who has seen each of the productions and can assess them, and the theatre space, in the context of many years' experience of British and foreign theatre. Lois Potter is a scholar with particular expertise in the seventeenth-century stage, who also knows and relishes modern performance. We have included a photographic reproduction of Trevor Nunn's unpublished Pre Show and Induction Scene for *The Fair Maid of the West*; marked up as a prompt book it will identify for readers

something of the complex activity of running a performance, and at least point towards the work of blocking and rehearsal. In casting our net so wide for contributors and topics we have tried to reflect the multifarious nature of theatre itself. We are nevertheless aware that some areas, lighting for instance and movement, are unrepresented, at least by separate treatment. If, in the end, the reader is more acutely aware of the kaleidoscopic variety of our arrangement, rather than any systematic order, we may perhaps claim that such variety represents quite faithfully the experience of theatre, at least until the ephemeral magic of performance draws it into temporary coherence.

Like theatre, the book depends crucially on its visual dimension. We have tried to complement the words of our contributors by a generous selection of photographs, plans and drawings, relating both to the theatre space and to its repertoire. The illustrations of the plays are static where performance is dynamic, but we have at least attempted to select material that shows the individual actor in spatial relationship to other actors, to setting and to props. We are especially delighted to be able to reproduce a selection of Sue Blane's costume drawings for *Every Man in His Humour* and *The New Inn*; though static, they imply in every line, as only the gifted artist's work can, both movement and, in a not unrelated way, character.

Since we embarked on this book, the Swan has been publicly recognised for architectural achievement by receiving a National Architecture Award of the Royal Institute of British Architects, and a Civic Trust Award. When contemporary architecture is far from universally in favour, and when a leading article in *The Stage* (8.12.1988) offers well-known actors' criticism of the failures of post-war theatre buildings, it is heartening to be able to celebrate a theatre which has drawn so much praise, both as building and as functioning performance space. The paradox of the Swan is that it is old and new at once, a true phoenix in giving new life to an existing building, and a phoenix too in freshly recollecting bygone performance spaces, without becoming in any way a pastiche — without indeed sacrificing the freshness of new architectural discovery.

This book has been brought together to complement an extensive exhibition devoted to the Swan, held at the Mead gallery of the University of Warwick in February and March, 1989. Through displaying a model and drawings of the theatre, and through the reconstruction of six shows from its first three seasons, making use of sets, costumes and properties, as well as lighting and sound, the exhibition evoked and paid tribute to the work of the theatre and the architecture of the space. The exhibition was originally conceived by Ronnie Mulryne and Margaret Shewring of the Graduate School of Renaissance Studies, and mounted under the direction of Katharine Eustace, Curator of the Mead Gallery. The exhibition designer was Helen Mallinson. In the preparation of the book and of the exhibition the ready co-operation of a large number of people proved invaluable. An acknowledgements page is included elsewhere in this book, but we should like to record here our very warmest thanks to many members of the Royal Shakespeare Company and especially to David Brierley, James Sargant, Brian Glover, Geoff Locker, Wayne Dowdeswell, Jenny Alden, Guy Woolfenden and Susan Davenport. The staff of the Arts Centre, University of Warwick, and of the Mead Gallery, together with the staff of the Shakespeare Centre, Stratford-upon-Avon (especially the Director, Dr Levi Fox and the Librarian, Mrs Marion Pringle) have put us in their debt by giving us every assistance. We are most grateful of all to those who have contributed so willingly, by interview or written paper, to this book. They have made it a pleasure to write it. Our final thanks are due to Mr Alec Jolly, Judith Boden-Cummins, Mr Kevin Hines and Mr Tony Waugh of our printers, Jolly & Barber Ltd, of Rugby, who with so much professionalism, good humour and patience brought this book into being.

Ronnie Mulryne
Margaret Shewring

The first Memorial Theatre in 1879 before the completion of the Tower

COURTESY OF SHAKESPEARE BIRTHPLACE TRUST

1 *From Conference Hall to Theatre*

TREVOR NUNN

Trevor Nunn *was educated at Downing College, Cambridge. In 1962 he won an ABC television trainee Director's Scholarship to the Belgrade Theatre Company, Coventry. In 1966 he became an Associate Director of the RSC and in 1968 Artistic Director and Chief Executive, a position he held until 1978, when he was joined by Terry Hands as Joint Artistic Director. Since 1965 he has directed over 20 Shakespeare plays for the RSC, and almost as many by other playwrights. In 1986 he resigned from Artistic and Executive responsibility for the RSC to pursue a freelance career. His productions since then have included* Cats, Starlight Express, Chess *and* Porgy and Bess. *He is currently directing* Aspects of Love *(a new musical with score by Andrew Lloyd Webber). In 1986 he was appointed Director Emeritus of the RSC. For the first season at the Swan he directed Thomas Heywood's* The Fair Maid of the West *(opened 11 September 1986).*

The first Memorial Theatre after the Tower was built (in 1888)
COURTESY OF SHAKESPEARE BIRTHPLACE TRUST

The development of the Swan came about gradually. Over a period of several years, actors and directors had demonstrated and articulated a great love of the building we rehearsed in called the Conference Hall. They felt comfortable working there and frequently complained that a tight and disciplined final run-through of a production in the Conference Hall became dispersed and disparate when it arrived in the Main Theatre. But it really took ages for it to dawn on me that this building had once been a theatre. Even though I knew that there had been a magnificent first Stratford Memorial Theatre which had burnt down in 1926, I never challenged the received idea that this auditorium had been 'razed to the ground' so I was inordinately excited to realise that the Conference Hall *was* the Stratford Memorial Theatre – pretty much complete and entire, just lacking the original roof. I began to investigate and discovered there was a box office area and a main foyer entrance, heavily disguised but still in existence, and that it *would* be possible to restore the building as a performance space.

So why did we need another performance space? We were constricted in our repertoire choices. We had a shared commitment – I think that all of the Associate Directors would have concurred – to presenting as many as possible of the works of Shakespeare's contemporaries, both to discover more of Shakespeare's context, and to educate ourselves, and because we were certain that there were all kinds of buried treasures to be uncovered.

But we were unable to carry through our commitment because of financial considerations – mainly box-office considerations. The audience which travels to Stratford from all over the world would consult their brochures and would say, 'but we are going to Stratford in order to see Shakespeare – so we must avoid the time when they're doing the Webster or Tourneur or Ford. We want to see Shakespeare.' So, our experience in the late 60's and the early 70's was that if we *did* try to put a non-Shakespeare play into the Main House repertoire, we suffered noticeably at the box office. The one occasion where that turned out not to be so was *The Revenger's Tragedy* in 1966. That was partly because the production cost the Company very little and therefore it was quite easy to justify financially; and partly, something about that play caught the public imagination because a production of *Hamlet* was in the same season. The Tourneur was a great critical success, and much comparison was made not only between the two productions (Peter Hall's *Hamlet* and my production of *The Revenger's Tragedy*) but of the two plays – and how one had clearly influenced the other and how there were both extraordinary differences and extraordinary similarities. So that experience was encouraging – and sufficiently successful for the play to be revived in the following season – but subsequent experience, for example, of doing *Malfi*, *Faustus* and *Women Beware Women* was much, much more difficult to reconcile.

Therefore as financial constraints at Stratford tightened, it became clear to us that the non-Shakespeare policy was a luxury we could no longer afford. So, not surprisingly, the alternative had to be to do such productions at The Other Place. There the box-office consideration was completely in reverse. We discovered that every time we did such a play there, we would have queues round the block – and there were hundreds of ticketless and infuriated patrons. We also realised that a production that had originated at The Other Place was very unlikely to be able to transfer to a larger space and maintain its integrity. All the physical reasons for the work being staged in a certain way would disappear.

Notoriously this was the case with *Macbeth*. That was a horrifying experience which became an object lesson. It was clear that such a transfer must never be repeated. That transfer took place entirely because of public demand – a demand that had reached dangerous proportions as far as the Company was concerned, with letters in newspapers saying the RSC clearly had failed in its responsibility to its public by doing such a demanded production in such a small space. There was a great pressure on me to do something about it. So I *did* transfer the production for a short time (to the Main House) with catastrophic results – bewilderment on the part of the general public who'd been led to believe that they were going to be very excited by it, and distress on the part of the Company who could no longer communicate *any* of the ingredients of the production in the Main House space. They felt betrayed – because they couldn't play at the scale that they wanted to for everybody who was close to the stage, and yet there was nothing in the production to enable them to communicate to the people who were much farther away. Clearly then, we couldn't take Other Place productions and scale them up.

So it was clear that there was both a repertoire demand and a continuing actors' and directors' affection for the Conference Hall space. I talked to John Napier about how a simple conversion might be achieved. To begin with I think I was being a bit pie-in-the-sky, because I was hoping that the space could remain a rehearsal room during the day and that bleacher seating of some sort could be pulled out from the walls so it could become a theatre that would seat about four hundred at night. John explored the idea and said, 'I'm sorry, it's impossible.' Instead, using the existing structure – including some huge pillars and a small balcony – John explored the nature of a Jacobean theatre not as conscious archaism, but in order to achieve with a promontory stage and a tiered auditorium that fundamental stage-audience relationship. (See page 8.)

John was an Associate Designer and this was at a time when there was no immediate work for him to do designing productions, so I gave him a six-month commission to work on the theatre possibilities of the Conference Hall. By the end of that six months there was a card model that I was able to show my colleagues – in particular, the General Manager, David

Brierley – and on that basis I took it to the Finance Committee of the Governors and eventually to the Executive Council of the Governors – who were intrigued.

I emphasised to the Governors that if we went ahead with the scheme it must not be thought of as an alternative to The Other Place – that it would be an addition. But, somehow – over the months – the briefing I gave on that subject was forgotten and at the point when fund-raising was to begin there was extreme alarm amongst the Governors when it was understood to be an additional space. 'Surely, he said it was going to be an alternative, and The Other Place would close down – and we'd do the work of The Other Place in the new building.' That was quite a high hurdle to get over. It was the support of Kenneth Cork and Dennis and Hersey Flower which won the final approval – they were not only fantastically loyal but visionary about the possibilities of the new theatre.

So the Governors gave permission for an architect scheme, and that's when I approached Michael Reardon, whom I knew, and who had designed the Riverside conversion. All of this coincided with the mounting of an RSC small-scale regional tour (the Ian McKellen company) when we did *Twelfth Night* and *Three Sisters*. Our first tour date was in the theatre in Christ's Hospital School, Horsham, a theatre designed by the architect responsible for the Young Vic. And *there*, pretty much in every detail, was the kind of space I was dreaming of.

Michael already knew of it and much of what John Napier had been exploring was similar in conception, but it was good to have an actual reference. Michael first of all designed an auditorium looking down on to a bare floor. If I remember correctly, I recall saying to Michael that I thought it was vital for there to be, however shallow, a platform promontory stage – that it *shouldn't* be a space that was confusable with or alternative to The Other Place, which is a one-room space, of a totally intimate nature, where works of introspection are thrillingly achievable. That's why productions of Chekhov, Ibsen and Strindberg there have been revelatory – because the necessity for projection is removed and therefore internal monologue seems to be the proper expression.

The Conference Hall space with its promontory stage and galleried auditorium is a public space, which has to be addressed, projected into, assailed – and I fear that when people attempt to use it at a lower level of energy, it won't work at all. Introspection contradicts the rules of the space and the dynamics of it. And even the geometry of it. Because the bulk of the audience is both surrounding and above the action, then the form of address must be outward and upward. It cannot be an address based on the idea that the audience isn't there. It can *only* be based on the acceptance that they *are* there, and they are welcome, that they are in some sense involved, they are acknowledged and used. They're not looking through a key-hole, not voyeurs – they haven't crept into a real event.

Michael made a beautiful, gem-like working model that was shown to Governors – amid great excitement – and this led to the approval for a fund-raising campaign. We tried approaching big firms and known beneficent individuals, with no success whatsoever. And then we decided to try our luck in America. The basis of the approach was that the

Americans had played a huge part in building the 1930 Stratford Theatre and here was an opportunity for Americans to play an equally huge part in building a sister theatre.

I went to America with Harold Wilson, the RSC president and the bait to get lots of phenomenally wealthy Americans to various dinners, where it was my task to stand up and make the detailed pitch. There was always great excitement, there was always much applause, and there was always not a cent. I mean nothing – absolutely nothing. The scheme felt to them, I think, to be too quaint, too expensive to be so quaint – and too remote – and there was no stirring of the conscience because we were a Company who already had a theatre and anyway the American theatre was in a bad state and in need of a lot of money, so why give it to an English Company? We failed completely.

The project was quite literally put on a shelf. That beautiful little architect's model was put on a shelf in the RSC Art Gallery in Stratford. Whenever I was asked about the scheme I made brave speeches declaring it was still a going concern – and that we were still actively seeking funding for it. Indeed once every six months I would write a letter or talk to somebody about funding the theatre, but the possibility was becoming more and more remote. Then the fairy story happened. An American philanthropist, Mr Fred Koch, saw the model in the RSC Gallery at Stratford. He asked an assistant some questions about it, was referred to the Curator, who referred him to James Sargant, who referred him to David Brierley, who referred him to me and about ten days later, I had a meeting with Mr Koch in London, giving him my by now very well-rehearsed speech. He was silent for a moment and then he said 'Well – this is something that I would like to do.' I said 'But in what sense would you like to do it?' He said 'Well – build it.' I said 'But we're talking about £1.5 million.' He said 'Well that's right – I'd like to do that, I'd like to pay for that.'

After that number of years, that number of attempts – and then it was *that* easy. Finally the project had found its benefactor. I was immensely tearful in the taxi going away from the meeting – I couldn't believe it and I was overcome.

But then something even better happened. We had been talking amongst ourselves where we could hire or what we could build in Stratford to be an alternative rehearsal room once the Conference Hall was no more and one day Michael Reardon said to me, 'The obvious place for an alternative rehearsal room is above the new theatre.' I said, 'Michael, we mustn't even mention that – it's much much too expensive a plan and I think we will be perceived as having misled the Benefactor if we go back to him with a much more complicated scheme.' Michael said, 'Well, let me work it out anyway.' His new scheme not only provided a handsome rehearsal space but restored the sky-line, the original roof-line of the first Stratford Memorial Theatre. It's not an exact replica but it rebalances the building and makes sense of the structure of the horseshoe-shaped brick building which until then had looked sawn-off and squat (see pages XII and 15).

So we *did* go back to Fred Koch with a revised scheme and he was absolutely marvellous. He said, 'It's just so much better a scheme than the first scheme that of course that's what we must do.' And he didn't blench at the *very* much greater cost that would be entailed.

The new rehearsal room above the Swan
auditorium.
PHOTOGRAPH: NICHOLAS SARGEANT

He said, 'Fine, I mean it has integrity and if it enables the Company to do its work better, that's what I want.' Such generosity is *very* rare and remarkable. Reluctant though I am to give credence to present Arts Council and Treasury beliefs that private enterprise can take over in huge measure from public funding, as far as nationally-subsidised organisations are concerned, it must be admitted that it was *only* by such private beneficence that the Swan could have been achieved.

From that moment on, I was determined that everybody in the organisation should know the *reason* and the *place* of the new theatre in the Company's ideology. I coined journalistic phrases – which make me shudder a little now, such as: it's where we're going to do the plays that influenced Shakespeare and the plays Shakespeare influenced; the repertoire will be the plays of 1570–1750 etc. They were short-hand statements, to give the public a handle on what we were doing. But they were phrases that reflected our passion to discover more, research more and present more of the Elizabethan and Jacobean theatre – and the theatre post-civil-war too.

My disappointment at present is that nothing has been done to include the works that influenced Shakespeare. I hoped that by *now* there would have been a production of *Magnificence* or *Everyman* or something like *The Old Wives' Tale* or *Gammer Gurton* – material that I think would work quite wonderfully in that space. I think the *first* season was correctly wide in spectrum. The plays came, as it were, from representative categories. I was determined that something from the Shakespeare Apocrypha would be included in the first year. We have to face the reality that these works are not ever going to be performed in the Main House, but it's appalling that the Royal Shakespeare Company with its Charter – and with its history – should have omitted such works from its repertoire where there is considerable evidence that Shakespeare had a hand – or influence – in the writing. So that is part of the academic or scholastic contribution that the Swan should make.

Such contributions should underline the position that Stratford deserves world-wide as the International Shakespeare Centre. It seems to me that if theatre in Stratford – geographically remote and expensive as it is – is going to survive at the highest level into the next century and beyond, then it must boast the very highest scholastic and educational credentials. Of course, what we have to do is to strike a balance. We must appeal to a regular theatre-going audience – to an average theatre-going audience too. There must be accessibility, even if it is a vogue word and one which supposedly theatre administrators should not be using in this elitist age. I think that Stratford theatre should be attractive and available to people of all backgrounds and all interests.

So, the first season opened with *The Two Noble Kinsmen* from the Apocrypha, and included a play of the greatest of the contemporaries, Ben Jonson. It's quite disgraceful that the RSC went *that* long doing so little Ben Jonson. We've started to correct it and it should now be statutory that a Jonson is done every year. It seems to me now that we have the Swan, that until the RSC has presented everything stageable and playable of Jonson – over the next ten year period – then a degree of shame will attach to the Company. To some extent, that

'This Golden Round': the interior of the Swan auditorium, from the stage.
PHOTOGRAPH: MARTIN CHARLES

should be true too of Marlowe. And there's still a cache of completely unknown plays – though known to *us* – we talk about them – we yearn to do them and they must get a hearing.

I'm a bit disappointed that in subsequent years after the first season the RSC have re-staged works that have been presented by the Company in the more or less recent past, but it was exactly right that the Swan prompted the re-discovery of *Hyde Park* and the renovation of *The New Inn*. But to repeat *The Revenger's Tragedy* and not do *The Atheist's Tragedy*, to repeat *The Man of Mode* but not do *The Wives' Excuse* has saddened me. I hear it is now quite likely that the number of Elizabethan, Jacobean and Restoration plays that will be done at the Swan each year may be reduced because of the enforced closure of The Other Place. So the choice of repertoire will become even more important and difficult than ever before. I can only hope the next few years will see the net being thrown wider and deeper so that those jewels do not remain all 'scattered at the bottom of the sea.'

Shakespeare Memorial Theatre: Conference Hall Interior *c*.1934
COURTESY OF SHAKESPEARE BIRTHPLACE TRUST

2 *Designing the Swan Theatre*

MICHAEL REARDON

Michael Reardon, M.A., Dip.Arch. R.I.B.A., has an architectural practice at Hillborough, near Bidford-on-Avon. In addition to his work as consultant architect to the RSC he is also consultant architect to the Dean and Chapter of both Birmingham and Hereford Cathedrals. He is inspecting architect to various parish churches in the diocese of London, Winchester, Coventry, Hereford, Birmingham and Worcester, and on the Planning Committee of the Council for the Care of Churches. He is a member of the Sandstone Conservation Study Group as well as Visiting Assessor at Sheffield University's School of Architecture. He is an occasional lecturer for the Architecture Association Conservation Course.

The idea of a third auditorium in Stratford, specifically for the performance of Shakespeare's contemporaries, had interested the Royal Shakespeare Company's directors for some years. In the 1970's, John Napier, a Stage Designer for the Company, modelled a simple galleried structure for this purpose which might be built within the Conference Hall behind the Main House.

After the destruction of the Old Memorial Theatre by a spectacular fire in 1926, the annual Shakespeare season was without a permanent theatrical home for some years, until the new Theatre was opened in 1932. The building was designed by Elizabeth Scott in an uncompromisingly modern style which we have now come to appreciate, but which earned it at the time the nickname of 'The Jam Factory'. Conceived purely as a proscenium theatre, it had always serious limitations for the production of plays which had been written for buildings like the Globe, and has been successively modified over the years.

The 1932 Theatre was built back to back with the ruins of the Victorian theatre, so that the scenery dock of the new theatre is built on the site of the stage of the old House – of which the auditorium walls and the lower part of the Great Tower survived, together with the Picture Gallery and Library which formed the foyer of the Theatre itself. (See page XII.) The surviving shell of the auditorium was later given a flat roof in place of the high pitched one destroyed in the fire. It was furnished as a Conference Hall, which eventually became the Company's rehearsal studio.

The brief, presented to us as Architects in 1979, was to create within this space a galleried structure which would seat some 150–200 people around the acting area, and which would be used exclusively for the performance of sixteenth- and seventeenth-century plays. The budget was a modest fifty thousand pounds, exclusive of the cost of providing alternative rehearsal space on another site. There was, from the first, no intention of treating the new theatre as an exercise in historic reconstruction. One cannot work in conservation without realising that buildings are of the age that created them, regardless of their designers' intentions. The best Gothic work of the 19th Century or the most careful reconstructions of classical antiquity may be masterpieces in their own right, but they do not deceive us as to their origin. Moreover, the painstaking reconstructions of one age will always be found lacking by the scholarship of the next, and it is likely that the proposed reconstruction of The Globe in Southwark, representing as it does the best knowledge of our own time, will be in dispute almost before it is finished.

The new auditorium therefore was not to be a reconstruction of the Elizabethan Globe or Swan, but a new performance space to embody some of the qualities those early buildings possessed, and which we believe to have enduring theatrical value. In particular, we wanted to re-create the relationship that exists between actor and spectator, when both are contained within a common architectural framework. We wished to re-create in modern terms, that is, the 'wooden O' of carpenters' work which formed, in such theatres, the ever visible framework of the play. Such a theatre represents a 'theatre of the word' in which the art of the actor takes precedence over that of the scene painter.

The parameters of the space were of course determined by the existing walls, but within these the concept began to evolve of an egg-shaped volume contained within three tiers of galleries, with an apron stage thrusting into the centre of it from one end. The resulting space would have a strong vertical accent and a feeling of emotional tenseness and concentration. Tim Furby's sketch to illustrate this concept brought an immediate and positive response from Trevor Nunn, and from this the whole design of the theatre evolved. The replacement of the rehearsal space, lost by the construction of the new auditorium, was a problem which we tried to solve at first on other sites, until we realised that the theatre would need a new roof and this could be designed in a form to accommodate the rehearsal space, which would be a very economic solution. Futhermore, positioning the rehearsal studio over the auditorium and within the same building as the Main House was administratively convenient for the Company, and economised in the provision of ancilliary accommodation and services. Dressing rooms and shower rooms, for example, would not have to be duplicated on another site.

An industrial sponsor had offered to support the project from its beginnings in 1979 and a start on site was planned for 1981, leaving an uncomfortably short period for the preparation of detailed designs and production drawings. A large scale model of the auditorium was made and working drawings were well advanced when the sponsor, with financial problems of his own, withdrew. A multi-national petroleum company then took on his role and the future of the project seemed secure, until the international oil crisis forced them to withdraw also. The completed model of the auditorium itself, however, was placed on display in the theatre's gallery – as a reminder of what might have been.

The story of the visiting American, who saw the model, asked why it was not being built, and, on being told the reason, offered to pay for the project, is now well known, nor is the Swan's generous benefactor any longer anonymous. The result was that, in November 1983, work on the project re-commenced. Our clients wanted the Auditorium completed, if possible, in time for the Bard's Birthday on the 23rd April 1986 – leaving us little more than 27 months in which to reappraise the design, execute production drawings and complete building works (see drawings on pages 12 and 13).

Work commenced on site in January 1985 and was complicated from the beginning by the discovery of voids in the existing brick walls of the Auditorium and by difficult ground conditions in the areas of new building. Much of the work had to be carried out whilst the Main House was in use, which meant that noisy operations could only take place within restricted periods of the day. Difficulties also resulted from the inability of some of the sub-contractors to work within the required programme and there were inevitably changes in both the scope and quantity of the works. In spite of this the first performance took place in May the following year, only 4 weeks after the original completion date, which perhaps reflects the enthusiasm and goodwill of all those involved in the project. The Theatre was formally opened by Her Majesty the Queen on the 13th November 1986.

In the auditorium, the acting platform, modelled on the forestage of the Elizabethan theatre, is surrounded on three sides with three tiers of galleries for spectators, the lowest of which is only slightly above the top level of the raked pit seating. At the stage end, the second spectator gallery is omitted and the third continues behind the stage and is generally used either for musicians or as part of the acting area. The fourth gallery goes round the entire space and is used for technical and lighting purposes, and from this two lighting bridges span laterally across the space. Lighting and sound control boxes are located at this top level facing the thrust stage. All the galleries are connected within the auditorium by staircases and may be reached from the stage area (see pages 6, 12 and 16).

Because of the restricted width of the auditorium, determined by the existing walls, the sight lines from the upper levels at the sides are very steep, and this means that the rear seats are elevated rather in the manner employed in the Manchester Royal Exchange. This is not a theatre in which you can lean back in your seat and 'wait for it to happen', but I find the way in which the audience hangs over the galleries and heads move to follow the actors' movements a positive aspect of the theatrical experience. Once they have accustomed themselves to the intimacy of this relationship, actors seem to like the feeling that their audience can almost be touched and are literally 'hanging on every word'.

The galleries, however, are not only a means to 'paper the walls with people' they are also the actors' territory, enabling them to make use of the whole auditorium on equal terms with the audience. There is no capacity for flying in the conventional sense, but a system of winches above the technical galleries allow odd props and even actors to be flown in and descents to be made. This facility, like the provision of stage traps is essential for the production of plays of those centuries. (See page 16.)

Of course the space has limitations, which may be regarded as disciplines or as disadvantages according to one's viewpoint. It would be difficult, for example, to construct and change an elaborate set. This to me is an acceptable problem, but the lack of space at the back and sides of the stage is certainly a disadvantage in some productions. This limitation was imposed by the relationship of the new theatre with the old, and could not have been avoided except by taking over part of the back dock area of the main house, which would not have been acceptable to our clients. (See page 12.)

The galleries are the dominating feature of the auditorium and the light-coloured wood and austere detailing of these were initially criticised by some people on the grounds that they were visually too obtrusive during the performance and the construction lacked 'period flavour'. The constant visual presence of this 'carpenters' work' is however an essential

plan ·· proposed

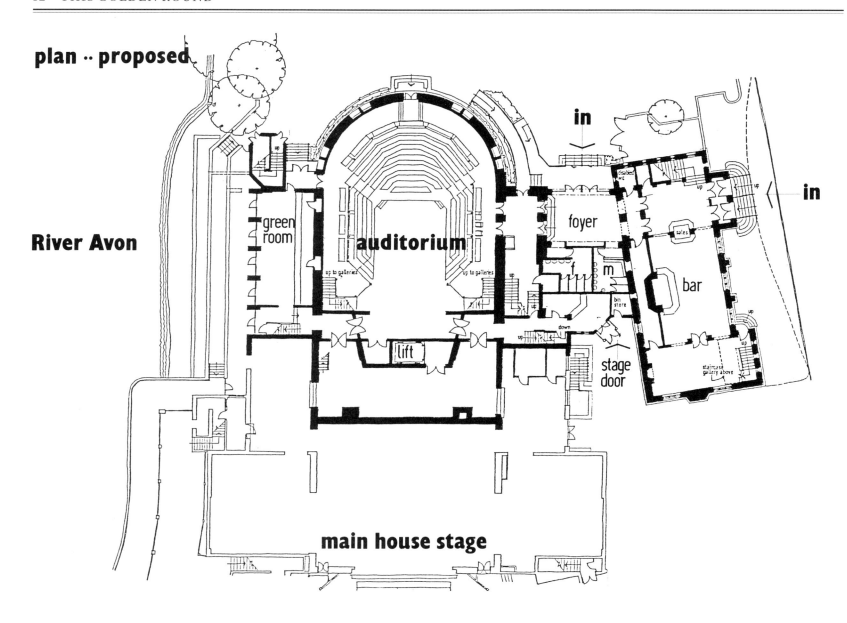

River Avon

component of the design, and absolutely intentional for reasons already explained. The choice of pine for their construction was suggested by the splendidly austere and unpainted reconstruction of the Teatro Farnese after war damage, and we deliberately wished to avoid any suggestion of half-timbered quaintness. In fact, the timber is now darkening naturally and is assuming a warm golden-brown colour.

The use of so much exposed timber for the structure of the galleries, however, caused

Courtesy of Michael
Reardon & Associates

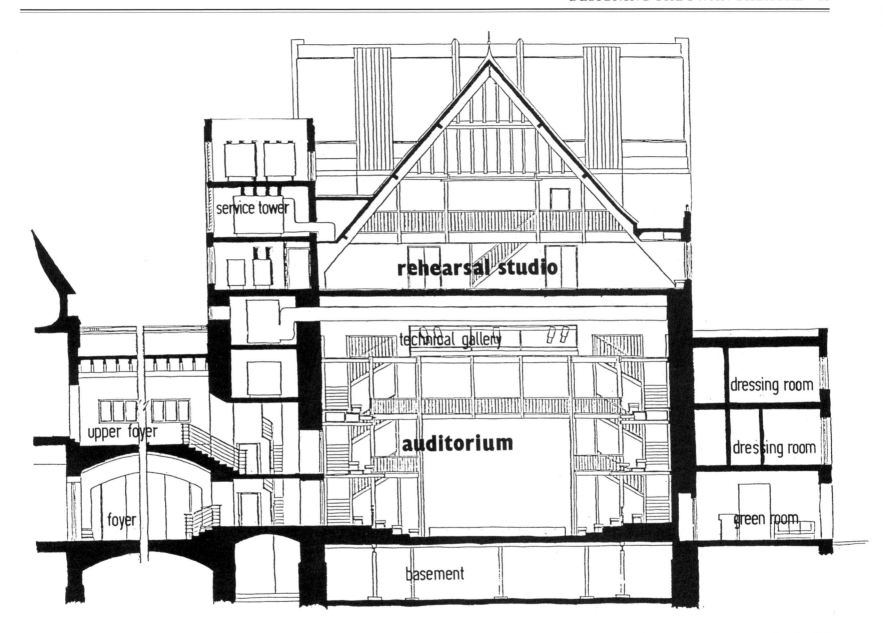

service tower

rehearsal studio

technical gallery

dressing room

upper foyer

auditorium

dressing room

foyer

green room

basement

Courtesy of Michael
Reardon & Associates

some problems in satisfying Fire and Public Safety Regulations. Requisite standards of fire resistance were eventually achieved by over-sizing some timbers and the general use of transparent fire retardant coatings. We had however to test one section of gallery front to destruction before the Local Authority Engineers were satisfied that they were capable of withstanding 'crowd pressure' without steel reinforcement. In the event they proved capable of withstanding two and a half times the required loading.

The stage itself is made of demountable rostra and can be removed to leave a flat trapped floor. There are, it is true, sight line problems when this is used as the acting area. The front seating rakes can also be removed, leaving a space in which the audience can stand, promenade or sit upon the floor. The stage rostra may also be used centrally with an audience on all four sides. In this arrangement, the omitted section of the gallery across the back of the stage may be put in. The auditorium is fully air-conditioned and has three routes of escape from the lowest level, with the majority of seats; and two from the other levels leading to protected staircases.

Acoustic quality, always difficult to predict exactly, has turned out well. The reverberation time is slightly longer than one might expect in a theatre but it is a resonant space which actors seem to enjoy using and music sounds well. There do not appear to be any dead areas.

The rehearsal studio which serves both the Swan and the Main House occupies most of the volume of the new roof. (See page 5.) The Gallery with its own staircase gives access to an actors' rest room at the upper level, which has a roof terrace overlooking the river. Below this are three floors of new administrative offices. The nineteenth-century Picture Gallery and Library, undamaged by the fire and subsequently used as offices, now form the foyer and bar of the new theatre. The upper floors house the RSC Collection of theatrical memorabilia, which the audience can tour in the interval.

The most prominent feature of the exterior is certainly the new roof whose shape is not dissimilar to the one destroyed in the fire, although it is differently clad and simpler in its ornamentation. In fact, there is no intention of imitating the old roof and its form developed naturally out of other considerations. When seen from the far side of the river, its form evokes the idea of a circus tent or a jousting pavilion – and this was intentional. The wind vanes, of burnished stainless steel, were designed by ironsmith Anthony Robinson, who said that he was inspired by the pattern of waves made by a swan swimming in the river. (See page 15.)

The bricks for the new work were hand made to match those of the Thirties building. The new brickwork had to be seen in juxtaposition with the Gothic revivalism of the gallery and auditorium, and the art-deco detailing of Elizabeth Scott's building. This made it difficult to decide what style should be followed. A study of the pattern of development since 1932 in which the Gothic core has been gradually enclosed within arms of new building in the latest style, offered a lead however, and we decided to base the new work on that of the Thirties and even to extend the truncated Gothic Tower (which now houses the air-conditioning plant), in the same style. This was criticised by the Royal Fine Arts Commission, but I think that it has worked perfectly well; and as a Cathedral Architect, I take a relaxed attitude to the juxtaposition of different styles in the same building.

The Swan Theatre has been designed for a specific purpose – that of performing sixteenth- and seventeenth-century plays, but there is no doubt that it is suitable for other purposes and certainly for the dramatic work of other periods.

The Royal Shakespeare Theatre from the river, showing the Swan exterior and the roof-line on the left.
PHOTOGRAPH: MARTIN CHARLES

Left
Stage set for *The Two Noble Kinsmen*
Shakespeare and Fletcher
Designed by Bob Crowley. This photograph, by
Geoff Locker, shows the cage (used to imprison
the two noble friends) and the trap-door.

Above
The Two Noble Kinsmen
Shakespeare and Fletcher
Arcite (*Hugh Quarshie*) and Palamon
(*Gerard Murphy*) in their 'prison'.
PHOTOGRAPH: DONALD COOPER

The New Inn
Ben Jonson
Sue Blane's drawings for the costumes of
Barnaby (*Laban Leake*) and Nick Stuff
(*Ian Barritt*).

3 Co-ordinating the Project

JAMES SARGANT

James Sargant *joined the RSC as Production Controller in 1971, and was responsible for the Company's move into the Barbican. Prior to 1971 he held a number of technical, design and administrative posts including rebuilding the Exhibitions at Madame Tussauds and mounting their Exhibition in Amsterdam. He has worked as technical director for the English National Opera. He is a director of the Tyne Theatre Company, Newcastle, as well as a director of the Tyne Theatre and Opera House, a member of the Council of the Association of British Theatre Technicians, and a director of the newly formed Oxford Playhouse Trust. With his wife, he owns and is a director of the Windmill Theatre, Newbury. He is currently Barbican Administrator and Tours Co-ordinator for the RSC. He was Project Co-ordinator for the Swan auditorium.*

After long years as the Conference Hall rehearsal room, it was at last agreed that the shell of the old Stratford Memorial Theatre should once again be opened as a working auditorium. The project was made possible by the generosity and foresight of Frederick Koch. As the person who had much of the early discussions and meetings with our benefactor, it was left to me to liaise with him on a regular basis. He was always more than understanding and constructive. He never interfered. Indeed, he constantly worked with us to achieve our goal.

Michael Reardon and his team, particularly his project architect, Reg Ellis, were untiring. They were determined to give us everything we wanted within the budget available, without ever imposing their ideas. They were always sympathetic. And once they set out on the track of solving specific problems or realising ideas they nearly always came up with solutions – which did not merely provide answers, but which improved the new theatre still further. It was an ideal dialogue and relationship.

One of the bravest decisions taken by the RSC, with the agreement of the architects, was to go ahead without engaging theatre consultants. One thing that made this a relatively easy decision was the knowledge that Michael Reardon had engaged Peter Jay as his services consultant – and he had extensive theatre experience. Another key factor in the decision not to engage theatre consultants from outside was our belief that sufficient expertise existed among our own heads of department and their staff. So it was a major decision from the outset that the RSC would be developing their own designs for the production lighting, sound and communication systems. As Michael and his team had to work against the clock in order to keep up to schedule with the working drawings required by the contractors, the RSC also took on the responsibility for building a temporary rehearsal room on The Other Place site. This was to make up for the loss of the Conference Hall as a rehearsal room until the new rehearsal room over the auditorium was complete. This relatively cheap and practical building has done sterling service, and is still in use at the time of writing, but scheduled for removal to satisfy the town planners in early 1990.

Lighting

John Bradley, the RSC's Technical Manager, undertook the design of the production lighting. As the Swan works with a very small technical staff – just two electricians – it was essential that all the lanterns could be reached without the use of ladders. This was no easy brief – and it was brilliantly realised. Sitting in the auditorium, although one can see all the light sources, none intrudes. The fact that the lanterns underneath Gallery 2 achieve this is thanks to Frederick Koch. When looking at the model, he remarked that it was a pity that the lanterns necessary in this position were so prominent, and, to a degree, broke up the clean and admirable line of the timber of the gallery fronts. The solution engineered by John Bradley not only gets over the problem, but has been admired by other theatre practitioners and has since appeared elsewhere.

Sound

Sound and communications were in the capable hands of John Leonard. Within a relatively small budget he achieved much. Although it was felt that the sound requirements of the space as a theatre would not be too demanding, we added to the brief the possibility that the Swan would serve as a conference centre from time to time. It was initially felt that this additional use could help the finances of the space, particularly in the Winter Season. Many extra facilities have therefore been provided and where wiring could not be afforded at least the routes for it exist. However, to date such use has been negligible. The success of the theatre as a performance space has meant that it has rarely been looking for other uses and its Winter Season has already gained a reputation of its own.

The 'inner stage'

Michael Reardon and I decided that it was not for him to design the division or screen between the main thrust of the stage and the rear stage area, which was intended to service the productions. We both felt that this was a design solution that might vary from season to season or even from production to production. In the final count this produced the most interesting outcome, in so far as the designers for the first season were so attracted by the quality of the rear wall and the extra depth of the 'inner stage' that they decided to leave it as it was. This did, however, produce problems both of very limited or virtually non-existent lighting positions in the rear of the stage area and of pushing the servicing of the productions into the sound lobbies separating the Swan from the main auditorium (and even into the backstage area of the Main Theatre itself). It was only in the third season that a rear stage area was to an extent being used as it was originally intended.

Directors and Designers

In the final stages of building, directors and designers at last began to show a real interest in the space they were going to have to use. And inevitably they immediately started to ask for changes, even by making direct approaches to Michael Reardon. But changes at that point were too late. Certainly they could not be afforded, and almost certainly they were not desirable. Virtually nothing was changed. Indeed, Trevor Nunn gave us great support by insisting that the company must use the space for the first season as it was designed as a process of discovery. Only then could changes be considered in the light of experience. How right he was!

The Team

The team who worked on the project for the RSC will for ever be left with a feeling of pride that so much was achieved in such a remarkably short time for such a programme of work – and, on the whole, so very successfully. As Project Administrator for the Swan, but still retaining some Barbican responsibilities, I will always be indebted to John Watts, who acted as the Project Co-ordinator and who lived with the problems of the theatre company and the contractor working together in a theatre still in full operation. He was ably assisted by John Bradley, and his assistant Simon Bowler, who had to keep services, plant, cooling and ventilation running against the odds.

The RSC Collection

One of the great joys of the project was to be able to incorporate all the spaces in the Gallery – now named the RSC Collection. These rooms had, of course, been the front of house facilities of the original Memorial Theatre. Brian Glover, as the Collection Manager, trod the very difficult path between excessive theatricality and making good use of the features of the interior; after all, the rooms may form part of the Collection, but they double as front of house for the Swan at performance times. There is not enough space to achieve either function, but what *has* been achieved has certainly revitalised the Collection, as well as providing one of the most interesting and colourful foyers in the country.

The Dream Come True

The fact that in the final count our target for opening was only missed by a month is a credit to all concerned. The problems on the way were considerable: ground so hard that the programme was almost six weeks behind before it had started; noise schedules that must have been the bane of the contractors' lives (but necessary to performances and rehearsals alike); one of the main gallery upright timbers needing to be replaced due to a split – no easy task; the extra requirements of the authorities brought about by the inevitable aftermath of the Bradford Stadium fire disaster and changes of local authority officers dealing with the project. We realised very late in the day that, in spite of endless sightline drawings, the view from the second row of the galleries was far from ideal – at which point the perch solution, as in the Manchester Royal Exchange, was introduced. But with the prospect in sight of one of the most exciting new theatre spaces for many a day, the impetus was kept going.

Indeed, one of the most astounding features of the whole project was the way in which one was still conscious of the remarkable atmosphere of a performance space at every stage. One never forgot that this was the shell of the original theatre. Nearly everyone believed that it was going to work and I am sure that its history as a building contributed a lot to this. This atmosphere is still very much there and seems to contribute so much to the unique actor/audience relationship of the Swan.

The Swan theatre is a dream come true, thanks to Frederick Koch's generous gift, and thanks to Trevor Nunn for the concept, and to Michael Reardon and Associates for the design that made the concept a reality.

The Two Noble Kinsmen
Shakespeare and Fletcher
Gerard Murphy as Palamon.
PHOTOGRAPH: DONALD COOPER

4 *The Repertoire of the Swan*

RONNIE MULRYNE & MARGARET SHEWRING

Ronnie Mulryne is Professor of English and Comparative Literary Studies and Chairman of the Graduate School of Renaissance Studies at the University of Warwick where he was Pro-Vice-Chancellor from 1982–1987. He took the degrees of B.A., M.A. and Ph.D. at the University of Cambridge and in addition to Warwick has taught at the Universities of Edinburgh and Birmingham. His publications include work on Shakespeare, Elizabethan and Jacobean theatre and W.B. Yeats. He is a member of the Drama Panel of the Arts Council, Chairman of the Arts Council Projects Committee and a Trustee of the Shakespeare Birthplace Trust.

The Royal Shakespeare Company's declared production policy for the Swan was to provide a stage for neglected sixteenth- and seventeenth-century plays including the Shakespeare Apocrypha – plays that may well have been popular in their own day but that have seldom or, in some cases, never been performed since. The appropriateness of the Swan to such plays derives not from any deliberate attempt at the antiquarian reconstruction of an Elizabethan or Jacobean playhouse, but in particular from the relationship of the promontory stage to the auditorium. Michael Reardon went for inspiration to the Teatro Farnese at Parma and to the Renaissance theatre at Sabionetta; he also drew on existing theatre spaces in this country. The three-tiered galleries of the Swan embrace the performance, making the costumed player the focal point and, as in the playhouses of Shakespeare's London, making scenic sophistication virtually redundant. Costume, combined with carefully selected visual images in the form of drapes, stage furniture and hand-held properties, allows the emphasis to be on actor, word and narrative, often requiring the audience to participate in the imaginative creation of the locations. The Swan offers, in other words, whatever its modern sophistication, a genuine re-creation of the essential playing conditions of the Elizabethan Swan, as represented in the De Witt sketch.

The production that marked the opening of the Stratford Swan was Shakespeare and Fletcher's *The Two Noble Kinsmen*, directed by Barry Kyle and designed by Bob Crowley. The play was probably first performed in the winter season of 1613–14 at the Blackfriars, and perhaps also at Court. With the exception of Davenant's Restoration adaptation, *The Rivals* (1664), no record exists of performances of *The Two Noble Kinsmen* from the mid-1620s until the Old Vic Company's 1928 revival with Eric Portman and Ernest Milton as Arcite and Palamon. Since then, only three professional productions have taken place in England.

Like the auditorium itself, Barry Kyle's production was in no way an antiquarian reconstruction. Shakespeare and Fletcher's collaborative piece, rooted in Chaucer's *Knight's Tale*, raises questions of chivalry and honour. Its values refer back to those of an aristocratic world of courtly love and noble deeds – a world in which the lady may be loved as a human being but may also be won as the prize in a tournament. Barry Kyle wanted to evoke in his staging a world in which such values would become comprehensible to a modern audience. After various false starts, he chose the world of the samurai, with its emphasis on physical prowess and martial skills as the outward signs of fitness of mind.

Emblematic patterns became a feature of the production, especially in the depiction of the chivalric world. Thus Theseus became the red-clad war-lord, whose conquest of Hippolyta was formally enacted in dumb-show at the opening: he shot an arrow into her breast, and as she fell he supported her and took rose petals from the wound. (See page 91.)

By contrast to the world of chivalry, the play offers the rustic life of the Gaoler, his daughter and the country-folk. This contrast was strongly evoked on the Swan stage. The red of Theseus' court gave way to the green and white costumes of morris dancers preparing for May-Day celebrations; and the ritual of formal conquest was replaced by a vigorous celebration of natural instincts and desires around a great leather phallus, that at one moment disgorged white silk over dancers and on-stage audience alike. (See page 79.)

Perhaps the most innovative decisions in the production related to the presentation of the two heroines, Emilia and the Gaoler's Daughter. Both find themselves in a world in which their natural instincts have to be subordinated to the codes of their social positions. Amanda Harris, in particular, portrayed Emilia as no more than a pawn in her brother-in-law's game, driven almost to distraction by her emotional predicament. She thus saw her as parallel to the Gaoler's Daughter, whose emotional vulnerability was so movingly portrayed by Imogen Stubbs. Barry Kyle's direction, which allowed for deliberate visual parallels between scenes with the two women, united the plots to offer a performance-coherence seldom previously thought possible.

The production was not to everyone's taste. Michael Coveney saw the piece as 'a ranting samurai cabaret broken up with laughable intrusions by ghastly rustics' (*Financial Times*, 12 May 1986). Others felt more in sympathy with Michael Ratcliffe's description of the production as 'marvellously clear, athletic, colourful and bold'. Ratcliffe went on: 'Bob Crowley's stunningly beautiful costumes – white, cream, black, saffron yellow and dramatic blood-red – are lit by Wayne Dowdeswell and set the play not in classical Greece but somewhere between Smyrna and Kyoto, in the romantic synthesis of Central Asia' (*The Observer*, 11 May 1986).

This opening production may be seen as pointing the way for others, not just in the choice of play, but in styles of presentation. The more formal, emblematic, and colourful patterning of the aristocratic court, with its emphasis on costumes, on silks, and on carefully-selected properties, can be thought of as anticipating the production style of *The Revenger's Tragedy* and *The Jew of Malta*. The energetic, rustic treatment of the Gaoler's Daughter and her social group – with its emphasis on movement and on the use of few scenic elements – looks forward, on the other hand, to the vigour of Jonson's *Every Man In His Humour* and *The New Inn* and to the celebratory, carnival worlds of *The Fair Maid of the West* and *The Rover*.

For some, the most conspicuous success the Swan has enjoyed has been in the presentation of the work of Ben Jonson. It has been said that in any other nation Jonson would be celebrated as a playwright of national significance. But the record of Jonson in the British theatre is dismal, aside from one or two remarkable productions such as Wolfit's *Volpone*

Margaret Shewring *is Lecturer in Theatre Studies at the University of Warwick and Course Director of the Graduate School of Renaissance Studies. She took her B.A. at the University of Birmingham and her Ph.D. at the Shakespeare Institute. She has published work on sixteenth- and seventeenth-century theatre and on the European theatre of the early twentieth century. She was Secretary of the Standing Committee of University Drama Departments from 1984–86. She is Co-Editor with Ronnie Mulryne of the* Renaissance Drama Newsletter, *the Shakespeare in Performance Series (Manchester U.P.) and volumes in the Warwick Studies in the European Humanities Series (Macmillan).*

and Bogdanov's *Bartholomew Fair*. Indeed, only a handful of Jonson's plays have received theatrical attention of any kind since the seventeenth century. As T. S. Eliot famously lamented: 'The reputation of Jonson has been of the most deadly kind that can be compelled upon the memory of a great poet. To be universally accepted; to be damned by the praise that quenches all desire to read the book; to be afflicted by the imputation of the virtues which excite least pleasure; and to be read only by historians and antiquarians – this is the most perfect conspiracy of approval.' It was such a 'conspiracy' the Swan set out to counter in the rehabilitation of little-known plays.

It was initially thought appropriate to open the Swan with a production of Jonson's *Every Man In His Humour*. The fact that it was presented second owed more to the logistics of Company planning and rehearsal time than to judgments of theatrical significance. In the event, *Every Man In His Humour* proved to be one of the Swan's most memorable productions, fully justifying the play's popular success at its first performance in 1598 (with Shakespeare listed among the principal players, probably taking the part of Old Kno'well). The stage history of the play through to the nineteenth-century productions of Edmund Kean and Macready, and the amateur production of 1845 in which Charles Dickens took the part of Bobadill, was one of continuing success. Since then, performances have been scarce, with the notable exceptions of Ben Iden Payne's 1937 production at the Shakespeare Memorial Theatre (with Donald Wolfit as Bobadill) and Joan Littlewood's 1960 Theatre Workshop production at Stratford East.

For the 1986 Swan season, John Caird and his company of actors used the 1616 folio text, much revised by Jonson himself from the 1598 quarto. They imported into it, however, some quarto lines, particularly in the closing scene of the play. Perhaps most importantly, as John Caird explains in a programme note, the 1986 version 'retained from the quarto Ed Kno'well's wonderful speech on the nature of true poetry, without which his character, his father's and their relationship to each other would remain sadly unresolved.'

Caird and his designer, Sue Blane, made a virtue of the intimacy yet strength of personality of the Swan auditorium. There were production challenges in plenty, particularly in the blocking of so intricately-plotted and episodic a play, with its multifarious stage actions and its multiplicity of characters and locations. The script is dense with references to properties. Notoriously, the language is verbally and syntactically complex, almost impenetrable for a novice reader. The machinations of Old Kno'well's servant, Brainworm, require numerous disguises, both verbal and physical. (See page 137.) But out of these challenges John Caird created an intensely energetic, visually strong and pungent production. Sue Blane's constant presence during rehearsals meant that she was able to offer costume designs that were not chronologically precise period-costumes but that were clothes appropriate to the individual actors, as well as evocative, rather than pictorially representative, of their roles. (See pages 57, 60, 92 and 93.) The stage was filled with specially crafted, solid furniture and props which felt real but were not in an antiquarian way authentic. These props and pieces of furniture were suspended, when not in use, on a series of ropes and pulleys in front of the rear brick wall, and from the side-stage galleries, conveying by their very presence the solid reality of a busy, merchant and working-class

London, without hampering the essential fluidity of the action. As Francis King remarked, 'the sterling merit of John Caird's production of *Every Man In His Humour* is that, so far from being deafened by the modern director's cry of "Look at me! Look at me!" one is hardly aware of his strong, capable hands at the puppet-strings' (*Sunday Telegraph*, 25 May 1986).

Many in the audience would have agreed with John Barber's assessment of the effect of the production: 'The drama became real life. I seemed to be back in the London of 1598 — drinking in the Windmill Tavern, witnessing a brawl, avoiding the blows a husband was aiming at his wife. Partly this is because the long platform stage is thrust deep into the midst of the spectators, so that the actors can button-hole you at one moment and mount a spectacle seconds later. Partly, it is because Jonson more than Shakespeare . . . employs "language such as men do use". And again, it's because in directing *Every Man In His Humour* John Caird identifies completely with his author.' (*Daily Telegraph*, 23 May 1986). Irving Wardle's review acclaimed the Swan itself as 'a matchlessly sensitive instrument for Elizabethan comedy', lending itself to 'highly detailed simultaneous action' so that 'the galleries allow a sense of busy London life going on in the background, while the forestage permits the greatest intimacy and speed of address'. (*The Times*, 23 May 1986.) The performances of Tony Church (Old Kno'well), David Haig (Brainworm), Pete Postlethwaite (Captain Bobadill) and Henry Goodman (Kitely) were universally acclaimed.

The following season, John Caird and Sue Blane tackled the even more formidable challenge of Jonson's late play, *The New Inn*, a play that has no record of professional revival since its unsuccessful performance by the King's Men at the Blackfriars in January 1629. There were divergent views among those who saw the Stratford production, or were involved with it. Some thought the play shallow and empty, others found it a moving testament from an ageing and disillusioned playwright. Few would, however, dispute the appropriateness of such a revival in the repertoire of the Swan, and no one doubted the success of Sue Blane's design. This complemented the structure of the theatre itself, exploiting its visual echoes of an Elizabethan inn yard to evoke, very vividly, the genial hospitality of the Host's Inn of the Light Heart at Barnet. Some members of the audience, visiting the Swan for the first time, even thought that the wooden staircase, extending from first-gallery level at the rear of the stage down to a small square landing, itself raised by a few steps from the platform, was a permanent feature of the building. (See page 94.)

If *Every Man In His Humour* represents Jonson at his most strenuous and most intricate, in terms of both verbal and dramatic syntax, *The New Inn* shows him constructing a fable that is relaxed intellectually and emotionally, perhaps even to the point of sentimentality. Michael Coveney responded to this by praising John Caird's sensitive direction which, he wrote, 'uncovers a glowing comedy of tavern life and romantic reconciliation that relates the play to the best RSC humanist traditions: *The Winter's Tale* meets *Nicholas Nickleby*. It also comes across as a near perfect resolution of the Jonsonian intellectual tension between learning and hedonism.' (*Financial Times*, 12 November 1987). Irving Wardle thought the play an 'energy show with a still philosophic centre' (*The Times*, 12 November 1987), a centre marked by the melancholy Lovel (John Carlisle) delivering two long speeches on Platonic Love and Honour in the presence of Lady Frampul (Fiona Shaw), the subject of his

The Rover
Aphra Behn
Carnival celebrations.
PHOTOGRAPH: JOE COCKS

infatuation. These speeches in the Court of Love Michael Coveney thought to be 'among the finest things Jonson wrote, and Mr Carlisle's delivery of them is electrifying'. Around this still point 'the stage swarms with above and below-stairs life (making much use of the trap), erupting into ludicrous deeds and wild pursuits with the slenderest motivation or none at all' (Irving Wardle). 'The company inhabits the play and the theatre (the two coalesce) with an irresistible relish, much aided by Sue Blane's glorious Caroline costumes, Guy Woolfenden's mellow song-settings and Wayne Dowdeswell's golden lighting' (Michael Coveney). The enjoyment of audiences of the two very different Jonson plays in the Swan repertoire seems to point to the peculiar suitability of that space for the performance of Jonson. It may be that we shall see future productions of some more of the less-well-known Jonsons, for example *The Staple of News* or *The Devil is an Ass*; the tension and isolation that *Epicoene* evokes should be particularly vivid in the Swan, during the 1989 season.

Where John Caird discovered the capacity of the Swan for representing the close-packed world of Jonson's plays, Trevor Nunn and John Barton found in it a freedom to create theatrical illusion with few props and the willing complicity of the audience. Trevor Nunn's production of a conflation into one play of two pieces by Thomas Heywood, recounting the adventures of Bess Bridges, the Fair Maid of the West, exploited this freedom wonderfully. For this production the Company used the simplest theatrical means, on an entirely bare stage, beginning the play with a fresh Pre-Show and Induction Scene by Nunn himself (see Appendix I). It emerged as a remarkably playable piece, which emphasised the illusionist nature of the stage and the collaborative nature of playing.

Not much is known of the plays' date of composition, nor indeed of their early performances or revivals, although Part One seems to have been popular during the Restoration. Since then, few productions are recorded. There was one by Stephen Kemble at the Haymarket in 1791, and one by the Phoenix Stage Society in 1920 at the Lyric, Hammersmith. A production for the Malvern Festival in 1932 was directed by Sir Barry Jackson.

As several contributors to this book emphasise, a successful performance has to take the Swan head on. Trevor Nunn achieved this by making his production an ebullient farrago of activity and colour. As he himself explains, this energetic comic-book fable of disguise, piracy and exotic adventures had proved attractive to him since student days. In his exuberant production, one was aware of the way in which a gifted choreographer of theatre, such as Nunn, could transform what seemed in the Jonson plays the strict and solid delineations of this stage into a free-flowing kaleidoscope. Michael Ratcliffe commented, 'Much of the play takes place in pubs or at sea, and John Napier (designer) transforms the open stage and the space above it with tackle, rigging, ladders and lamps that suggest equally tavern and ship. A low balustrade around the edge protects the spectators when the gallants flash steel and the pewter begins to fly.' (*The Observer*, 28 September 1986). John Peter took this further: 'The writing is warm, briskly heroic, fast-moving and undistinguished. Nobody has anything so complicated as an inner life: the emphasis is on action and the abrupt turns of fortune. Foreigners are devious and brutish but susceptible to instruction; Englishmen are brave, resourceful and loyal. English women are brave too, as well as desirable, and moral to the core' (*Sunday Times*, 28 September 1986). Trevor

Hyde Park
James Shirley
Julietta (*Felicity Dean*) and Trier (*James Fleet*).
Designer, Gerard Howland.
PHOTOGRAPH: JOE COCKS

Nunn explains how the casting of Imelda Staunton as Bess Bridges was crucial. Her ability to put a distance between her own appearance and personality and the fantasy heroine she presented ensured that the audience remained constantly aware of the theatricality both of the piece and of its manipulation of the stage space. Nunn's whole production was a triumphant vindication of the capacity of the Swan, in the hands of a skilled director, to free and not restrict a play's rhythms. (See pages 58 and 59.)

Some of these same qualities of freedom and vitality were evident in John Barton's production of *The Rover*. Aphra Behn's play drew the interested attention of potential audiences because of the reputation of the authoress as a feminist. *The Rover* is, however, a remaking by Behn of an earlier play, and very little about it, as with other of Behn's works, could be described as feminist in character. The play is, as Behn herself acknowledged, much indebted to Thomas Killigrew's *Thomaso; or, the Wanderer* (1654; published 1664) which, in its turn, draws on earlier works (including Middleton's *Blurt, Master Constable*). *The Rover* marked the Swan's first venture into plays from the Restoration years: Behn's play was first performed at the Dorset Garden Theatre on 24 March 1677, in the presence of Charles II (with Thomas Betterton as Belvile, his wife, Mary, as Florinda, and Elizabeth Barry as Hellena). It remained extremely popular on the London stage for a full century, but then, with the exception of an adaptation entitled *Love in Many Masks* (Drury Lane, 1790) seems to have disappeared from the performance repertoire.

John Barton's 1986 revival was itself an adaptation, drawing on Aphra Behn's theatrical palimpsest but incorporating even more of the Killigrew play and rewriting some of Behn's original work. As Barton explained in a programme note, 'about 550 lines have been cut and some 350 added'. Yet this extraordinary mixture held as an abundantly entertaining evening in the theatre. The exoticism of an already exotic narrative was intensified by Barton's decision to set the play in an unspecified Spanish colony, rather than in Spain itself, and to make Belvile into a black soldier of fortune (played by Hugh Quarshie). Angellica's role as a famous courtesan was also much extended (played by Sinead Cusack).

Audiences at the Swan accepted the improbabilities of the plot because of the sheer colour and activity of the performance. What might well have been regarded by feminist spectators as sexual treason seemed forgivable in the atmosphere Barton and his designer, Louise Belson, deliberately invoked. With its masked figures and disguised roles, and the prevailing sense of impropriety and sexual risk, high spirits counted for more than sexual politics. (See pages 27, 111, 150 and 153.) Guy Woolfenden's carnival music filled the air. The playing of Imogen Stubbs (an actress for whom questions of sexual identity and gender politics are of consequence) infused into the role of Hellena a carefree attitude appropriate to, and allowable in, the carnivalesque atmosphere of frivolous reversals of values. Her performance, skilfully balanced against Jeremy Irons as Willmore (The Rover), provided a sexual chemistry that gave the production a human tension at its core, and served to hold together the disparate events.

By contrast, two productions from the 1987 repertoire demonstrated the theatre's capacity for expressing the intense emotionalism of much Elizabethan and Jacobean playwriting:

Tourneur's *The Revenger's Tragedy* (directed by Di Trevis) and Marlowe's *The Jew of Malta* (directed by Barry Kyle).

The Revenger's Tragedy is celebrated among Jacobean plays for its exaggerated relish of grotesque and sexually-charged situations, to the extent of earning from T.S. Eliot the censure that it was the product of a sick and adolescent mind. After its early performances by the King's Men, probably in 1606, there is no record of production until a semi-professional revival in 1954 (in London). Since then, there have been a number of productions both in England and the United States (where a 1970 production by the Yale Repertory Theatre claimed to be the first American professional revival). In 1966, Trevor Nunn directed the play for the Royal Shakespeare Company in the Main House in Stratford (transferring to the Aldwych in 1967), with Ian Richardson as a coldly calculating, meticulous Vindice, manipulating his enemies in a black-clad, silver-masked court.

Antony Sher played Vindice in 1987 'like a cornered rat' (John Peter; *Sunday Times*, 13 September 1987). Eric Shorter compared the production unfavourably with Trevor Nunn's: 'It may . . . have been that such evil is easier to manage effectively on a "picture-frame stage" than at the cosy Swan, where we are too close to events and seem to share the same room as the actors who tend to come and go through it' (*The Daily Telegraph*, 15 September 1987). But many shared Michael Ratcliffe's pleasure in this outrageous revenger: 'Sher takes to the smaller theatre with evident pleasure, and his revenger is powered by wit, a sense of injustice and a terrible, violent joy' (*The Observer*, 20 September 1987). Di Trevis felt the need with her designer, Michael Levine, to transform the appearance of the stage — even its geometric configuration — into a place of risk and threat. The characteristic lightness and warmth of the Swan was veiled and muted. In the gloom even the promontory stage was made precarious by tilting part of it in the fashion of a broken-legged table. (See page 81.) The visual order of the gallery fronts and the rear-stage brick wall were masked by dark, torn hangings, obviously concealing inner chambers and hiding places for intruders. Against this background, the costumes and wigs were extravagant: 'dusty, gaudy, deliquescent, hoar-frosted with sequins and cheap glass, rotting into the wearers' skin'. (See page 80.) In such a costume, Lussurioso (Nicholas Farrett) seemed 'a jewelled ginger fox' (Michael Ratcliffe). The charged grotesquerie of this world was presented to the audience in such emphatic close-up that there was no escaping its violence: 'the poisoned skull is operated by Sher as if it were a ventriloquist's property' (Michael Coveney, *The Financial Times*, 14 September 1987), while Phil Daniel's Bastard took delight in 'mocking the rhetoric of his betters, picking each word off like a scab' (Michael Ratcliffe).

Di Trevis explains elsewhere in this book how the tense and stilted movement, evoking the sense of an acute awareness of threat, was expressed in the choreography of Jane Gibson (Movement Director). One had a sense throughout the performance of the face beneath the mask, the skull beneath the face, the putrid skin beneath the clothes — all contributing to the sense of corrupt lust beneath a veneer of court privilege and social manners. Jane Gibson shared with Di Trevis a vehement distaste for the corruption of power politics, and a strong anger at the subjection of women in such a venal and manipulative world. She had recently worked with Shared Experience, on that company's adaptation of Zola's *Nana*, where some of the same contradiction between social veneer and personal vileness made itself felt. There movement and dance were again used to help to convey this sense of a corrupt world.

Antony Sher's Vindice had an arrogance and edgy vehemence that made him an apt denizen of the world of *The Revenger's Tragedy*. He made his first appearance crawling from beneath the stage to emerge through the trap like some disturbed animal, clutching the skull of his long-dead fiancée, Gloriana. He soon discarded his hermit-like sack-cloth, however, for an aggressive, punk outfit. (See page 125.) This, combined with a bright scarlet Mohican hair-style, gave visual expression to the obsessiveness of the revenge-motif, as well as to his situation as an unrecognised outsider at court – fit to be both pander and murderer. His self-assumed role was appropriate to the theatricality of a world in which all the characters wore their costumes as disguises, in order to cover their sordid desires. Where Jonson's characters were rooted in a reality that could be described as domestic and every-day, Tourneur's characters inhabit a vividly fantasticated world. This difference was marked in Di Trevis's production by the economy of the properties – a skull, daggers, nothing more. *The Revenger's Tragedy* made excellent use of the claustro-phobic set, with its threatening proximity to the audience, to convey a dangerous, not a liberating, theatricality – a theatricality constantly underlined by throw-away cynical lines and grotesque humour.

Where Eliot regarded *The Revenger's Tragedy* as adolescent in character, he granted to *The Jew of Malta* a maturity which expressed itself in terms of 'savage farce'. From the play's early performances, probably in 1589 (with Edward Alleyn as Barabas) it continued in the popular repertoire into the early 1630s, but then disappeared from stage records until, in 1818, Edmund Kean starred in an adaptation of the play by Samson Penley (Drury Lane). Marlowe's play was not further revived until 1923 (The Phoenix Society at Daly's Theatre, London). The quatercentenary of Marlowe's birth, in 1964, saw a scatter of productions, including one directed by Clifford Williams for the Royal Shakespeare Company (which began at the Aldwych and was re-cast for its transfer to Stratford Main House in 1965, when Eric Porter played Barabas in tandem with Shylock).

The stereotype of the Jew is a particularly difficult one to handle on the modern stage, because of the intensely emotion-charged associations it carries. As Michael Billington argues: 'it is useless to deny that Marlowe submitted to the anti-Semitic prejudices of his time. But it is equally clear that he adored Barabas for his energy, craft and excess' (*The Guardian*, 16 July 1987). Sean French saw the need for an appropriate performance style, pointing out that Barry Kyle 'correctly judged that Christopher Marlowe's grand guignol can only be made to work theatrically if it's played as a crazy comedy.' (*The Observer*, 19 July 1987.) Indeed, Kyle's innovative solution was to rebalance the play's anti-Semitic bias by his treatment of Machevil. For where, traditionally, Machevil – with his links with the devil and political scheming and corruption – is associated with Barabas, Kyle chose to have John Carlisle double the parts of Machevil and the Christian Governor of Malta, Ferneze. This shift in alignment to some degree freed the audience from both the Elizabethan stereotype of the evil Jew and the modern stereotype of the suffering Jew, while allowing the production to demonstrate that the whole society of Malta was permeated by the self-seeking greed which it is all too easy to associate with one race or creed within that society. Kyle also found a way of releasing the play from the more debilitating kinds of quaintness which can easily serve to distance plays of the Elizabethan period. His Jews were not of the sixteenth century, but of any century (dressed in the black garb of the orthodox Jew); his Knights of Malta wore the timeless white robes and red-cross of St John associated with their order; his Turks were Arab terrorists, armed with machine guns; Bellamira, the prostitute, listened to a ghetto-blaster. The effect of all this de-periodization was to increase the accessibility of the play but also, somewhat, to dilute its grotesquerie and black humour. (See page 127.) Alun Armstrong's Barabas became a theatrically zany *tour-de-force*. 'He makes the character a consummate role-player, weeping into his kerchief at the maltreatment of his race before snapping out of it to get on with some villainy and at one point turning up disguised in straw boater and tricoloured garters like a Gallic George Formby.' But, as Michael Billington adds, this engaging performance lacked 'the element of grandeur and the sense that the character is obsessed by revenge' (*The Guardian*, 16 July 1987).

The production worked well on the Swan stage, which offered the intimacy necessary for Barabas's asides, while proving itself capable of sustaining a production full of elaborate scenic structures and stage devices. As Irving Wardle writes: 'This is a piece that calls for spectacular staging, and Bob Crowley (the Designer) has risen to the challenge. Besides the fiery pit, he supplies a tower of packing-cases which opens up into the rooms of Barabas's house, whence issues showers of gold, and which finally unhinges into the diabolical drawbridge for the final trap. After which, accompanied by (The Composer) Ilona Sekacz's sardonic variations on ''Ave Maria'', and surmounted by an image of the Virgin, it undergoes its last malign transformation into a cathedral' (*The Times*, 16 July 1987). Like the scenery, the props had a pictorial value rather than solidity. Indeed, if some felt that the stage-world evoked by Barry Kyle's production lacked savagery, it certainly exhibited the vivacious anarchy of farce.

By contrast, Isabella Bywater's design for Deborah Warner's un-cut production of *Titus Andronicus* (1987) was characterised by the art that conceals art. (See page 114.) This strong-sinewed production presented the only single-author Shakespeare play so far performed at the Swan. Among recorded stagings of *Titus Andronicus* (mainly, but not exclusively, confined to the second half of this century) was Peter Brook's celebrated 1955 production at Stratford, with Laurence Olivier as Titus. Brook's production made use of a colourfully expressionistic stage design in what is now the Main House. Deborah Warner chose, rather, to exploit the plainness of the Swan, in order to intensify the starkness of the fable, while releasing a sense of the human suffering the play so patently evokes. The whole production was supremely restrained – what Brian Cox describes as at once 'eipc and intimate' and, hence, fully in keeping with the Swan itself (see page 113).

As Michael Coveney wrote, 'in his second large scale performance of the season, Mr Cox has a field day as the war hero who turns plaintiff in his own land before feigning madness and playing the role of a sadistic revenger. Much of what makes *Titus* a going concern for audiences today is its underlying question of how best we express grief, and its challenge to our capacity for horror' (*The Financial Times*, 14 May 1987). Most remarkable about this *Titus* was the sense of human suffering conveyed through the simplicity of stage design, costume, sound and blocking. The figure of Lavinia in a simple, off-white, shapeless garment was almost constantly present, and the spoliation of the human body became a matter of intense pathos as, in the intimacy of the Swan auditorium, Lavinia's stillness and enforced silence became at once human and iconic (see page 115).

The visual austerity of this production was in marked contrast to the flamboyance of *The Fair Maid of the West* or *The Rover*, and to the idiosyncracy and individuality of *Every Man In His Humour*. The effect was to make the human figures emblems of suffering, setting them off (as in the Elizabethan theatre) against the unchanging, natural wooden backdrop of the auditorium itself. This was the Swan in its character as a genuinely empty space – making available the potential for a living theatre, with its emphasis firmly rooted in language and character, not in spectacle. Trevor Nunn explains elsewhere in this book his reasons for *not* casting a black actor in the black role of the King of Fez in *The Fair Maid of the West*, because of his conception of that play as deliberately flamboyant, carefree, theatrical. In Deborah Warner's *Titus Andronicus* the casting of Peter Polycarpou, a black actor, in the role of Aaron (the Moor) endorses the fully human emphasis throughout. Paradoxically, this production brings the extravagances of Shakespeare's Ovidian script to the test of human feeling. Indeed, it may be that one of the most viable characteristics of the Swan is to permit the counterbalancing of eloquence with restraint, large gestures with subtlety of expression. As Michael Billington notes, 'Ms Warner's wiliest tactic is to pre-empt possible laughter at the play's grosser cruelties by launching them in a spirit of dangerous jocularity . . . Even the final cannibalistic banquet stills our nervous laughter precisely because Ms Warner prefaces it with servants merrily whistling like the Seven Dwarfs as they set up the tables and usher in the dubious feast' (*The Guardian*, 14 May 1987).

One criticism which has been voiced concerning the auditorium is, in some people's eyes, its undue tendency towards elegance and visual refinement. The mannered world of James Shirley's *Hyde Park*, here transferred in Barry Kyle's production from its Caroline setting to the world of the Bloomsbury Group in the years leading up to the First World War, might have been thought to be particularly appropriate to such a stylish auditorium. Yet, perhaps because of the shift to the twentieth century, Kyle's designer, Gerard Howland, thought it necessary to superimpose what was virtually a proscenium-arch structure onto the rear portion of the stage – dividing, as it were, the artist's studio and the elegant drawing room from the outdoor world of the Park itself. (See page 28.) Kyle's choice of period was carefully thought through. *Hyde Park* was probably first performed in 1632 by Christopher Beeston's company, Queen Henrietta's Men, at their Phoenix Theatre (or Cockpit) in Drury Lane. It retained its popularity until 1639, and was revived during the Restoration (July 1668; Theatre Royal, Drury Lane), but there is no record of subsequent revivals until the 1987 Swan production. The play, therefore, belonged to the years prior to the collapse of social structures, and monarchy, in the Civil War: years when the extravagances and excesses of fashionable society had become self-consciously mannered and, sometimes, bizarrely 'progressive'. Kyle found a parallel in the self-consciously intellectual Bloomsbury group, before the onset of the ugliness and savagery of the First World War. The self-regarding posturing of character and language was echoed in the stage design, with its use of reflective columns (like proscenium-arch pillars) and its careful placing of exquisite portraits. Indeed, the whole play is no more than a series of games and deceptions played out to counter the boredom of polite social and sporting occasions in the Park: a cross between *My Fair Lady* and *Gigi*, in which costumes and manners take precedence over human emotions and values. Against this background,

The Man of Mode
George Etherege
Harriet (*Amanda Root*) and Sir Fopling Flutter (*Simon Russell Beale*).
PHOTOGRAPH: JOE COCKS

Mistress Carol's outspoken and awkwardly gauche flaunting of the expected role of the mistress was played by a deep-voiced Fiona Shaw — exciting both amusement and admiration for her daringly satiric and outspoken attitudes and her somewhat cynically dismissive neglect of the fashionable presentation of self. Many would agree with Francis King's surprise that, under Barry Kyle's direction, 'this absurd comedy proves far more entertaining . . . than one would ever have expected' (*The Sunday Telegraph*, 19 April 1987).

The policy of rehabilitating little-known plays continued into the 1988 season, which was given over to three plays from the Restoration period and to Edward Bond's contemporary piece, *Restoration*, based on the manners of the late seventeenth century. Such a policy ought perhaps to have matched the Swan auditorium with appropriate plays, those written for the playhouses of the early 1660s – for converted tennis courts with deep apron stages thrust out into the audience, and galleries enveloping them on three full sides. These playhouses offered an intimate indoor space of a comparable capacity to the Swan. Unfortunately the plays chosen belong to a later era: William Wycherley's *The Plain Dealer* and George Etherege's *The Man of Mode* (both 1676) and George Farquhar's *The Constant Couple* (1699).

The Constant Couple, as directed by Roger Michell and designed by Ultz, was by far the best adapted to the Swan stage. The overall impression was of a luminous, light golden world (the stage was even covered with a paler wooden overlay) fully appropriate to a society based on decorum, civility, and refined good taste. The light, optimistic atmosphere was further complemented by exquisitely crafted models of London buildings of the last decades of the seventeenth century, attached around the front of the first gallery. (See page 40.) These had the effect of embracing the whole auditorium within the world of the play. The culmination of this motif came with a splendid model of Christopher Wren's St Paul's, with its architectural decorum and aspiring lines, rising centre-stage through the trap.

The productions of *The Plain Dealer* and *The Man of Mode* were, for many, only moderate successes. They sat uneasily in the Swan, with sets designed to imitate the proscenium arch stages of the later Restoration years, masking the natural structure of the Swan auditorium with white stage drapes in *The Plain Dealer* (see page 37), or cutting off the rear-stage with a series of matt-black hinged panels, for *The Man of Mode*. What *The Man of Mode*, along with *The Constant Couple* and *Restoration*, revealed was the variety and complexity of a Restoration stock character normally dismissed as a mannered fool – the fop. Simon Russell Beale discovered true depth and variety in his portrayals of Sir Fopling Flutter, Clincher and Lord Are. There were few other notable successes among the characterisations; the sense of uneasiness that affected the staging of the plays seemed to communicate itself quite widely among the Company – although confidence grew as the season progressed, and the mannered language became more familiar.

The experiment of staging a full Restoration season certainly justified itself, offering an opportunity to see a range of rarely-performed plays and allowing each to be illuminated by juxtaposition with the others. This permitted the Company to build an increasingly detailed picture, not just of such social types as the fop, but of the hard-bitten yet fashionable world of the last decades of the seventeenth century: a world in which reputation took precedence over personal morality and social identity took precedence over matters of conscience. There can be little doubt that it would be worth repeating such an experiment in the future, though with a more appropriate selection of plays to complement the possibilities of the auditorium. Meanwhile the following discussions, by Lois Potter and Simon Russel Beale offer more detailed assessments of the successes and failures of the Swan's 1988 season, both from the point of view of a scholar and of an actor with the somewhat daunting task of 'playing the fop'.

The Plain Dealer (opposite)
William Wycherley
Directed by Ron Daniels and designed by David Fielding. Eliza (*Jaye Griffiths*), Novel (*Mark Hadfield*) and Olivia (*Joanne Pearce*)
PHOTOGRAPH: JOE COCKS

The Plain Dealer (page 38)
William Wycherley
Manly (*David Calder*) and Freeman (*Oliver Cotton*).
PHOTOGRAPH: JOE COCKS

The Man of Mode (page 39)
George Etherege
Harriet (*Amanda Root*) and Mr Dorimant (*Miles Anderson*).
PHOTOGRAPH: JOE COCKS

The Constant Couple
George Farquhar
Sir Harry Wildair (*Pip Donaghy*) and Colonel
Standard (Tony Armatrading).
PHOTOGRAPH: JOE COCKS

5 *The Restoration Season*

The Relevance of the Restoration

LOIS POTTER

Lois Potter *is a graduate of Bryn Mawr College, U.S.A. and took her doctorate at Cambridge. She is editor of Volumes I and IV of* The Revels History of Drama in English *and has published* A Preface to Milton *and* Twelfth Night: Text and Performance *as well as an edition of* Paradise Lost, *Book III and* The True Tragi-comedy *by Francis Osborne. She frequently reviews play productions for* The Times Literary Supplement.

The RSC evidently learned something from the fact that the biggest success of the Swan's first three years was a Restoration comedy, Aphra Behn's *The Rover*. Audiences, it appears, do not on the whole go to revivals of plays they have never heard of. 'Restoration comedy', however, has an acceptable public image: however immoral the goings-on, they will at least be presided over by well-dressed people. The logical conclusion was to turn the Swan entirely over to Restoration romps, and the season's opening production, Farquhar's *The Constant Couple*, gave every reason to suspect that this was going to happen. The play provides happy endings all round, with minimal gestures toward verisimilitude on the one hand and morality on the other. In retrospect, one can see that it was written, so to speak, in inverted commas, and the Swan production matches its self-consciousness with deliberately outrageous costumes and over-the-top performances. Contrary to what some reviewers suggested, Roger Michell's direction was also sensitive to other tones in the play. Pip Donaghy made Sir Harry Wildair a genuine eccentric, not just another dashing rake, and the female characters were sympathetically treated: Maureen Beattie and Jenni George succeeded surprisingly well in making something touching out of Lady Lurewell's improbable story of her lost love.

Even so, there was perhaps some element of playing for safety in opening with this essentially lightweight play. But audiences who came back for the Wycherley and Etherege pieces expecting more of the same certainly did not get it. To its credit, the company, instead of simply exploiting its audience's preconceptions, built on and modified them. The decision to round off the season with Edward Bond's *Restoration* must undoubtedly have affected the way in which the directors of the three 'period' plays approached them. In particular, the servants' roles, normally taken for granted in Restoration productions, received an unusual degree of attention, suggesting an awareness of that secret world of bewildered and largely doomed social defiance with which Bond's play is concerned. There was no attempt to gloss over the immense importance of money to all the characters. Above all, though this is not to take away from Simon Russell Beale's well-deserved personal success, the fop parts he played benefited enormously from this juxtaposition. If Bond's Lord Are seduces audiences into approving of his heartless wit because it reminds them of less critical depictions of a similar type, Etherege's Sir Fopling Flutter and Farquhar's Beau Clincher acquire a context, and a subtext, which their authors deny them. In short, the plays are held up for critical inspection rather than being turned into a playground for fantasies about an age of unlimited extravagance and sexual freedom.

The two plays with which I am concerned here, *The Man of Mode* and *The Plain Dealer*, were produced within a year of each other: the former probably on 11th March 1676, the latter on 11th December 1676. All the evidence indicates that much of their attraction, for their first audiences, lay in what was perceived as their truth to the reality of the contemporary London scene. Though Etherege himself, characteristically, makes no direct statement as to his intention, the friends who wrote the prologue and epilogue to *The Man of Mode* comment on the realism of its depiction of the fop. Neither dwells on something which must have been of even greater interest to the first audiences, the identity of Dorimant. He was generally thought to be a portrait of a real person, the Earl of Rochester, who was a friend of both Etherege and Wycherley. In this respect, the play has much in common with Behn's *Rover*. The latter was based in the first instance on the self-indulgently autobiographical play, *Thomaso*, by Thomas Killigrew, manager of the rival King's Company; Behn, however, renamed her hero Willmore, possibly as an allusion to Rochester, whose family name was Wilmot. The actress Elizabeth Barry, who played Willmore's partner, Hellena, in *The Rover*, may also have been the first Loveit in *The Man of Mode*; at any rate it soon became one of her parts. She was also Rochester's mistress, and was said to have owed much of her early success to his careful rehearsing of her. Thus, *The Man of Mode* is ultimately a flattering play, because it gives the audience information which is withheld from the characters, and allows them access to a private, backstage world.

Wycherley's play deals with very recent history. There had been two wars with the Dutch in Charles II's reign, but the play probably alludes to the more recent one, from 1672 to February 1674, which would have been of personal interest to many members of the audience. His play includes a discussion of his own *Country Wife*, all the more complicated in that it is based on Molière's dramatised discussion of his own *Ecole des Femmes*. Moreover, Wycherley, unlike Etherege, surrounds his play with his own commentaries. The prologue was written for Charles Hart, the actor who created the role of Manly. It assures the audience that they themselves are the models for all the unpleasant characters of the play, while only the honest hero and the happy ending are fictitious:

> For where else, but on stages, do we see
> Truth pleasing, or rewarded honesty?

Those spectators who find virtue boring and are unwilling to believe in such characters as Fidelia will find the author and actor only too willing to agree with them. At the same time, that agreement is turned back on them when Hart/Manly urges, 'If not to th'honest, be to th'prosperous kind'. In other words, by applauding the ending, which unexpectedly rewards the hero with a faithful and wealthy wife, the audience can simply show its usual readiness to back the winner without committing itself to any unfashionable approval of honesty.

In the end, both plays were performed without their prologues, though the one to *The Plain Dealer* was spoken in the preview performances and only cut later to save time. After all, no amount of direct address to a twentieth-century audience is going to turn it into a seventeenth-century one. But, curiously, one effect of the season was to draw attention to the continuity between Restoration drama and the Elizabethan–Jacobean drama for which the Swan was originally designed. The theatre has the long apron stage, with entrances at the back, characteristic of the period before the civil war; none of this season's directors attempted to find an equivalent for the sliding shutters and wings which made up the scenery of the Restoration stage. The positioning of the doors at the back is reflected in the common situation of Elizabethan–Jacobean drama where some characters make entrances from behind others. Usually this results in the characters at the front of the stage commenting on those just entering ('look where he comes'). In Restoration plays, on the other hand, the characters who enter (through doors on the front platform) are more likely to spy on the ones already there (defined by their position within or in front of a 'scene'). At the Swan, the directors generally placed the observers behind those observed, rather than between them and the audience, thus perhaps losing something of the complicity between actors and spectators which the plays invite.

It is possible, however, that Etherege and Wycherley were themselves still thinking, at times, of the pre-war unlocalised stage where there was no need to explain or motivate entrances and exits because much theatrical space was by definition open to all. One feature of both plays is an emphasis on the difficulty of having any privacy even in one's own home. In *The Man of Mode*, most of the characters seem not to mind living in public: Dorimant receives visitors while dressing, and Lady Townley is happy to have her house used as 'a general rendezvous'. On the other hand, this public life can be inconvenient, as when Dorimant's friends interrupt him just after his seduction of Belinda. Sir Fopling's arrival at Lady Townley's in masquerade annoys the other guests, who tell him that the country dance for which they have hired fiddlers was meant as a private party. In *The Plain Dealer*, the tavern in which Oldfox is able to tie up Widow Blackacre in a private room, is, paradoxically, a more private place than anyone's house seems to be. Manly has trouble keeping people out of his lodgings, even with two sailors guarding the door; he, Freeman and Fidelia are able to walk straight into Olivia's drawing room and eavesdrop on her without anyone noticing; Olivia's and Vernish's attempts to seduce Fidelia are constantly interrupted.

The sets for the two productions coped in different ways with the demands of this public world. Ultz's set for *The Man of Mode* told one nothing: it was a black background full of concealed doors and slashed with gaps through which lights occasionally shone, creating a sinister twilight world in which characters were constantly spying on one another. The furniture in the indoor scenes was kept to a minimum. No one has imposed his or her personality on a room. Even the outdoor scenes brought no sense of freshness or relief; the characters don't go to the Mall to admire the trees, but to see who else is there. Yet, against this ugly and modernistic background, the characters wore handsome period costumes in sober colours. In *Roscius Anglicanus*, John Downes, the prompter at Dorset Garden, commented that 'This Comedy being well Cloath'd and well Acted, got a great deal of Money'. The stress on clothes, and the absence of any comment on the 'scenes', is significant. Thus, the production emphasised the sense in which the characters are forced perpetually to create their own identities by means of clothes – as Dorimant, in the first scene, is observed gradually building himself up, layer by layer, into an irresistible rake. By contrast, David Fielding's set for *The Plain Dealer* was elegant but grandiose and empty-looking. The rooms seemed much too large for a private residence. The walls were white, the pillars were white; there were even dust sheets (white) on the chairs. Perhaps the intention was to confirm Manly's sense of society as a whited sepulchre. Westminster Hall was indicated by a green carpet stretching across the stalls area of the auditorium, thus allowing (even though this scene was one of those most heavily cut) for something of the procession of fools that Wycherley wanted.

Because the characters live so completely in public, there is little sense of an inner life except what can be conveyed between the lines. This, I think, explains the longstanding controversy over the plays' heroes and the actors playing them – who, interestingly enough, were also those most heavily criticised by reviewers. Miles Anderson as Dorimant was felt not to be attractive or charming enough; David Calder as Manly was too genial and too old. Each director, it would appear, had deliberately cast and directed the central role so as to counteract audience preconceptions. The graceful language of *The Man of Mode* has always tempted readers to imagine wistful melancholy behind the polished exteriors of its characters, especially Dorimant. *The Plain Dealer*, on the other hand, is usually seen as crude and two-dimensional in comparison with its main source, Moliere's *Misanthrope*. But Garry Hynes directed *The Man of Mode* so as to frustrate audience desire to know more of the characters' feelings than they themselves express, while Ron Daniels sought to humanise Wycherley's characters as much as possible.

Dorimant's success as a rake is essential to the plot of his play, and it is reinforced by the chorus of willing or unwilling admiration which surrounds him. The problem, as Garry Hynes evidently saw it, is to prevent the audience from surrendering to his charm and overlooking the extent of his ruthlessness. In this production, the scenes between him and his discarded mistress Mrs Loveit (Marie Mullen) were so highly charged that they cast their shadow over his courtship of other women. The most striking quality of Miles Anderson's Dorimant was self-control, taken to an extreme which was admirable but not sympathetic. Even in his brief asides to the audience and his conversations with his friend Medley, there was never any sense that we were being given an intimate glimpse of a vulnerable human being behind this mask. His rages with Loveit had themselves been planned in advance, as was clear from his conversations with Medley. Belinda at times seemed to represent the experience of the audience, when she realised that, despite having been forewarned of Dorimant's character, she had nevertheless allowed herself to be seduced by him. Harriet, who proves herself his match, did so by proving herself equal to him in both self-control and cruelty (Amanda Root caught this very well in her treatment of her mother and of Loveit). On the other hand, the most frank and honourable young people in the play, Young Bellair (Mark Sproston) and Emilia (Jenni George), are self-conscious and unglamourous. Young Bellair's dissembling, in his famous scene with Harriet, may not seem very different from hers, but they develop in different directions in the course of the play: she becomes an even better hypocrite than Dorimant, whereas he turns out to be far less in control of his image, and indeed, not very different from his old-fashioned father. The fact that they are in love with the same woman suggests the essential likeness between them. (Old Bellair's courtship of Emilia is the one real embarrassment of the play, and the production refused to palliate its awfulness.)

Mocking the older generation for their coarse habits is simply a way in which the younger generation of the 'town' attempt to carve out an identity for themselves. The same is true of their treatment of the fop, a character type no less fascinating for its original audience than for those at the Swan. The year 1676 was only the climax of an absorbing interest in dress and foppery which can be traced from the start of the Restoration era. But a further reason for the ambivalence toward Sir Fopling is that his foppery takes the particular form of Frenchification. Even the word 'mode' is a sign that fashion is French, and the Frenchified fop is ridiculed in other plays, such as Wycherley's *Gentleman Dancing-Master* (1672) and James Howard's *The English Monsieur* (1674). As early as 1661 the diarist John Evelyn had published a pamphlet, *Tyrannus, or the Mode*, in which he argued that a nation's political independence was related to its cultural independence, and that the copying of French fashions was a form of slavery. At a period when Parliament was busy enforcing religious uniformity, he urged the king either to regulate court dress by reviving the old sumptuary laws or to establish a single uniform fashion. In October 1666 the king actually tried this experiment — Evelyn attributed it to the influence of his little book — and Louis XIV, recognising the anti-French sentiment behind the gesture, promptly dressed all his footmen in the same style. The experiment was, as Evelyn later admitted, 'too good to last.'

Just as the Swan showed Restoration characters on a basically Jacobean stage, it also showed them balanced between the native English pastimes of pre-war years and the more refined ones that have come in from the continent. The stage direction at the beginning of Act IV of *The Man of Mode* calls for the characters to enter as if they have just completed a country dance. Garry Hynes directed the scene so that it opened with the dance itself — a rowdy, old-fashioned affair, yet one in which Dorimant as well as Old Bellair can comfortably take part. After Dorimant's departure, Sir Fopling suggests that they sing the new *bacchique*. This is a word which Old Bellair has never heard of, but it turns out to mean a catch, which both men are equally able to sing. On the other hand, Sir Fopling's singing and dancing are emphatically un-English. Simon Russell Beale happens to be a good singer; thus, his rendition of his epigrammatic French-style song gave the lie to Dorimant's rude comments about him. Trying to have it both ways, the other characters ridicule both the fop's French affectations and the fact that he is not always quite accurate in his imitation of them. But they themselves occupy a stylistic limbo, and the production hinted that refinement is rather a strain for many of them. The veneer is definitely slipping, for instance, in the early morning scene at Dorimant's house, which showed all the men except Sir Fopling sprawled awkwardly about the room and Young Bellair, in particular, barely able to keep up the genteel manner.

The lack of refinement of the high society depicted in *The Plain Dealer* was even more obvious, and it clearly took some critics by surprise. John Peter, in *The Sunday Times*, actually accused Ron Daniels of coarsening the play by making the fops so noisy and by having Olivia spit to indicate her disgust. The spitting is in fact indicated in Wycherley's own stage direction, and the noisiness is commented on by other characters. Indeed, Wycherley's prologue indicates the effect he was after:

> *His men of wit and pleasure of the age*
> *Are as dull rogues as ever cumbered stage.*

Ron Daniels treated Wycherley's unlikely collection of grotesques as sympathetically and realistically as possible. This was particularly true of the women. Eliza (Jaye Griffiths) is attractive and witty; Fidelia (Geraldine Alexander) was the more sympathetic for being neither of these things; Widow Blackacre (Marjorie Yates) was an intelligent eccentric rather than the usual pantomine dame, while even the appalling Olivia, as played by Joanne Pearce, won a little sympathy simply because, far from being a clever schemer, she was so thoroughly stupid in all her attempts at evil. But even the male characters (apart from Vernish, who seems unsalvageable) emerged from this treatment with unsuspected psychological depths. That Manly should be an elderly if vigorous soldier made sense of his naivety about women and justified the director's emphasis on his self-disgust after his sexual deception of Olivia (something of which the text itself gives no indication). It also helped to explain the attraction he holds for Fidelia, whose wealth, we learn at the end, is the result of her father's recent death. That she should be searching for another father figure helps to explain the uncritical nature of her adoration for a man whose name implies not only courage but *machismo*. Freeman (Oliver Cotton), despite his apparent kinship with the usual Restoration rake, is obviously most comfortable in Manly's company and pursues a woman whose sexual demands can be specifically excluded by a legal contract.

In its probing of motives, as much as in Garry Hynes's stress on their ultimate unknowableness, *The Plain Dealer* mirrored the national identity crisis of the period in which it was first produced. Manly's whole sense of himself is bound up with the idea of plainness and openness. Yet he himself is forced to become a dissembler when he realises that he is still in love with Olivia in spite of her betrayal, and he brings the entire cast to be witness of his final exposure of Olivia, just as Dorimant wants 'the town' to observe his humiliation of Loveit and her humiliation of Fopling. He thus falls into the same pattern of behaviour which characterises the others: secret intrigues contrasted with public spectacle. His military career has already manifested the same sense of division against himself. We are told that he blew up his own ship to keep the Dutch from taking it, and he is almost as rude to his own sailors as he was to the enemy. It is evident from his surly manner that he should never be fighting the Dutch on the side of the French; similarly, he seems to be making the wrong allies in his private life. He is rude to Freeman and Fidelia, the two people who seem genuinely eager to help him, while falling for the phoney Olivia and Vernish. It is only at the end of the play that he makes peace with them. Wycherley's own relation to his sources reflects the love-hate relationship with France. It's significant, I think, that the one idealised character in the play, Fidelia, comes from an English source (*Twelfth Night*), while the fops and flirts are based on French models. Yet Manly's identity, like Dorimant's, ultimately depends on France. He would have, literally, no existence without the previous existence of Molière's Alceste.

The two plays, then, depict a society caught between role models, at a time when, at the insistence of Parliament, Charles II was being forced into a public break with France and an alliance with Holland, while simultaneously maintaining secret links with France and receiving an annual subsidy from Louis XIV. An audience in the 1980s, though unaware of this context, may perhaps detect the resemblance to the current uncertainty about Britain's national identity in relation to Europe and the United States. More important, perhaps, is the contemporary uncertainty about social and sexual freedom. Terry Hands's *Man of Mode* in 1971 reflected a period when the general view was that everyone should have as much sex as possible and that anyone who wanted to spoil this process (Mrs Loveit, for instance) was simply ridiculous. That particular party is over, and the relevance of Etherege's play now comes from his depiction of the darker side of the liberated society, and the disquieting extent to which success depends on the ability to put on an act. Even in *The Plain Dealer*, the fools and villains suffer, not for their hypocrisy, but for their inability to sustain it. All that these plays need to make them completely relevant to modern society is more explicit reference to the fact that half their characters are suffering from sexually transmitted diseases.

There is one final point about the effect of seeing these plays, or indeed any plays, in the Swan. As regular attenders of this theatre have learned, the nature of the experience depends, to an astonishing extent, on where one happens to be seated. Crucial scenes of *The Man of Mode* are sometimes played so far downstage as to be visible only to the central section of the audience; watching *The Plain Dealer* from the side means that one is eavesdropping on the play much as many of the characters are. The directors were blamed for the poor visibility, but it is hard to see how any conceivable blocking could have enabled every member of the audience simultaneously to have a full view of important nuances of expression. Partial and imperfect perception of the plays thus seems built into the seventeenth-century theatre experience. Going to the same play more than once, as Pepys and others did, must have been not merely a social custom but an absolute necessity for anyone who wanted to understand it properly. Given the time and the money, I should have been happy to do likewise. Both the plays and the productions are complex and interesting enough to deserve it.

Playing the Fop

SIMON RUSSELL BEALE

We started the series of Restoration plays at the Swan Theatre with *The Constant Couple* by Farquhar. When the cast met for the first reading, Roger Michell, the director, insisted that the play was simple, bright and optimistic. He had an image of the young playwright arriving in London from Ireland and finding a confident, substantially rebuilt city that was careering into a new century of rationality and relative calm. Whether this was true is irrelevant, the image was useful. The play was peopled with characters with names like Lurewell, Wildair, Smuggler, Standard, and therefore the actors could not shy away from the simplicities that their functions within the piece and their names implied. Funnily enough, the character I had been given to play had a name and a function that were not very easy to pin down. He was called Clincher – I still don't know quite what that means – and was obviously, for want of a better description, the low-life comic part. He and his brother were played in the original production by two famous comedians of the day. So, above all, he had to be funny. As one of my fellow actors, Joe Melia, who was a marvellous Touchstone, said to me, 'Laughs are too precious to throw away.' If I may give an example. Very early on in rehearsals, I noticed that Clincher Senior has a soliloquy – and I mean a real one, not plot-laying, not an aside, but an expression of what he feels and thinks. He's been thrown into Newgate prison and is waiting to be hanged. Soliloquies are not what we associate with fops – Sir Fopling Flutter has none – in fact he has only one aside. Here, however, in Clincher's soliloquy was a chance to look inside a fop's head. So the director and I decided to play it very seriously. Deadly serious lighting, not a laugh in sight. By some people it was admired as something of a *coup de théâtre* by the director – and indeed it is very dramatic. *But* after some time, it became evident to all of us that we were forcing the text to do something it didn't want to do. If I wanted to move the audience or at least make them sympathise, then I had to be a little more delicate with my brush-strokes. I've ended up with one moment when Clincher breaks down in tears – the rest is comic. What I'm trying to say is that, as in all comic parts in classical plays (especially the simpler ones like Launcelot Gobbo or the Clown in *The Winter's Tale*), one has to *earn* the serious moments. Only when one has fulfilled to the fullest extent one's comic function, can one turn the audience's response inside out.

I have to confess that having played the Clown in *The Winter's Tale*, I have a chip on my shoulder about people's perception of the process of playing comic parts in classical plays. The substance of these parts lies in the performing of them, and in the personality of the performer. I think that almost anything is allowed in the process of turning often archaic and sometimes incomprehensible language into something that is amusing for a modern audience. The funniest and the best Porters in *Macbeth* that I have seen had an improvisatory quality that absolutely fulfilled the function of the part. I realise this is heresy, but I do believe that our job, especially in the RSC, is not to perpetuate a type of heritage theatre, a danger that a national company is particularly prone to. It's interesting to note incidentally that both the seventeenth-century fops I'm doing lose the interest of the playwright in the final scenes, once their comic function has been fulfilled.

To return to *The Constant Couple* and Clincher. Because I was doing three fops in a row, I felt I had to return to very basic questions. Why does a fop feel the need to behave as he does? Does it stem from a feeling of inadequacy or perhaps a type of super-confidence? Is the exaggerated behaviour they display the result of stupidity or rather an intelligent, defensive action? Should it be seen as a threat by others in the play or just as merely silly? I also started asking the wrong questions – like 'How do I make three fops different?' In the case of Clincher, I took the simplest and the obvious course. I hope it's supported by the text, or rather, I hope I'm not distorting the text. Clincher affects what he sees as fashionable behaviour out of a sense of inadequacy, and out of a desire to emulate those whom he admires. He is in fact a poseur. For this he is punished and he changes – not dramatically, but he changes – 'I've lived like a fool and shall die like a knave.' Simon Callow – a great player of fops – said once in a TV show that fops are essentially survivors.

This is not exactly the case with Clincher Senior. Farquhar presents a view which is easy for a modern audience to understand – that what a man is inside is what counts. This is very different from Etherege and his attitude towards Sir Fopling, as I hope to show. The similarity between Sir Fopling and Clincher is that they both have a child-like, perhaps even childish quality, but that's as far as it goes. Clincher emerged from rehearsal with the clumsy physical mannerisms of an over-enthusiastic child, dressed with no other desire than to make a splash, and with aspirations that are destroyed to the satisfaction of everyone.

The Man of Mode was an altogether more difficult experience. We made a lot of mistakes – although they were mostly to do with our use of the space rather than with characterisations. The set has presented a problem – both technically and artistically; and the decision not to use the downstage exits has limited possibilities. However, work on Sir Fopling Flutter proved to be fascinating and productive for both Garry Hynes, the director, and me. The first thought the director threw at me was that perhaps Sir Fopling was rather *good* at what he does. Perhaps he's genuinely elegant, perhaps the comments from those around him (he's 'pert and dull, brisk and insipid') stem from other motives than a desire to assess accurately another person. I must stress this was the first idea, not a picture of the final product. Consequently, our designer, David Ultz, decided to dress Sir Fopling as beautifully as possible. One critic wrote after seeing the show that the men's costumes showed differences that would only be evident to the eye of a Sir Fopling. He meant it as a criticism, but had obviously failed to see the point of David's designs. Instead of dressing Sir Fopling as an outsider (in the usual frills and flounces), David saw him as a chic extension of an already chic world – the sort of man who wears five buttons on his cuff rather than three. His real problem is that his *effort* is all too evident – nonchalance is about the only thing he can't affect. Having got an idea of what he looked like, it was impossible now to play him with the same lack of self-knowledge, and perhaps lack of intelligence that had been Clincher's particular weakness. Obviously, Sir Fopling's motives for adopting this high-risk social policy were different. I suspect that Sir Fopling is, at the very least, a little more intelligent than he appears. I know that during rehearsals Miles Anderson, who played Dorimant, saw Sir Fopling's grace and apparent self-assurance as some sort of threat. He saw Sir Fopling's behaviour as a challenge, because Sir Fopling assumes that he is the leader of whatever group he chooses to join. In the great scene towards the end of the play, when Dorimant and Mrs Loveit finally try to pick through the wreckage of their relationship, most of the talk is not about them, but about the position of the fop in their society. Firstly, according to Mrs Loveit, fops are not a threat to women because they are not remotely interested in women as sex objects. Secondly, with fops, what you see is what you get – a type of remote, social doll. Dorimant, on the other hand, is a liar – because he invests in his relationship with women and simultaneously pretends not to. Sir Fopling does not care about or want any of the women he comes into contact with. In the final analysis, I think Sir Fopling's behaviour is probably a self-defensive and intelligent choice. Or rather, he decides that the world into which he was born gives him *no* choice – you're either a Dorimant (whose behaviour has its own type of risks) or you disappear into the background like Medley, or, most excitingly and least dangerously, you become a fop, and preferably a good one. The only risk you take is that people – mostly other men – will laugh at you. Sir Fopling is, I think, well aware that Dorimant and his friends think him ridiculous, but he chooses to ignore it. We found that this gave him both a ruthlessness and a dignity that made him more than just a comic turn – a real survivor, in fact.

There is a qualification to this argument however. It was arrived at by accident in rehearsal. There is a scene, again at the end of the play, in which Sir Fopling sings a song. The four men involved are drunk and tired; it's six o'clock in the morning after a long party; Dorimant has just thrown Belinda out of his apartment. It turned, in one afternoon, into a scene where the similarities between the four men – Medley, Dorimant, Bellair and Sir Fopling – became very evident. It also became a scene when tiredness forced Sir Fopling to drop his act and consequently to display something of his loneliness. The song – though trivial – seemed to me to represent absolutely accurately the nature of Sir Fopling's existence: 'I drive about the park and bow, still as I meet my dearest.' The director asked if I would sing it as seriously and as well as I could. It has become a tiny moment of genuine expression of feeling from Sir Fopling – and, true to form, he leaves the stage before he gives anything more away. When he reappears in the last scene, he's back to his old self, and finally disappears off without having suffered any change or sustained any hurt.

Lord Are, in Edward Bond's *Restoration*, hardly comes into the category of fops. In fact, at one point, he denies firmly that he is one – not that *that* proves very much. The difference between this character and the other two lies firstly in Are's malevolence and secondly in the extended political function that he performs in Bond's version of the eighteenth and twentieth centuries. Are's principal motive in life is to trivialise all that happens to him. He is passive and his passivity is reinforced by his position in society. What is fascinating for me as a performer is that his part is, in effect, a long one-sided conversation with the audience. Not an extended soliloquy or even a detailed analysis, but an anecdotal stream of witty or savage comments. Like Richard III, I suppose – and, like Richard III it requires a great, even if manufactured self-confidence. Lord Are hardly performs within the play, at all, in the sense of talking to the people around him. As an actor and as a character you have to regard the audience as your friends. It is this particular performance quality in Are that Bond uses to such extraordinary effect when the going gets tough, in the second half of the play. Are uses his close relationship with the audience to involve them directly in the exhilaration he feels at the discovery of his own power. A lot of criticism has been levelled at Bond's writing of this section of the play – in fact at his desire to write a serious attack on the rich and powerful. If the play were in any way a simple picture of the wicked aristocratic master versus the put-upon peasants, then to me it would still be a viable statement that would deserve dramatic expression. But it's so much more than that. This government – and indeed any Tory government in this country – can still push legislation through the House of Lords by calling upon what I think are called backwoods-men – hereditary and politically passive peers who still have political power should they choose to use it. Lord Are, born to a position where he has never had to think about the power he unconsciously wields, discovers that he can do more than sit back and wait – though given his position *that* would do him no harm. He discovers, and for him it's an exhilarating moment, that when he decides to act, the repercussions are greater than he

The Constant Couple
George Farquhar
Sir Harry Wildair (*Pip Donaghy*) and Clincher
Senior (*Simon Russell Beale*)
PHOTOGRAPH: JOE COCKS

could ever have hoped for. *And* he asks the audience to congratulate him on his discovery. That seems to me to be a pretty powerful political statement. As to Bond's writing in the second half of the play – yes, the laughs don't come crowding in at the rate they do in the first half, but that, in itself, doesn't make it any less watchable or interesting, and it certainly doesn't, in itself, make it more 'political'. So many people who came to see the show felt that because the first half is funny and the second more serious, then they have been, in some way, 'conned'. I'm not sure whether they mean that when they laugh they don't have to think, or whether they see no political substance in the first half, but either way it doesn't seem a very powerful criticism of Bond's writing. By the way, I don't think that the play is perfect. The songs are trite and clumsy, and really should be cut.

The importance of Bond's play in the sequence that I have performed is that it has changed my opinion of the scope that seventeenth-century fops offer to the actor. Lord Are is a man given political power. Sir Fopling does not want political power and Clincher probably wouldn't know what political power meant. But, instead, the two seventeenth-century fops have a driving egomania that Lord Are discovers only half-way through the play – and that type of egomania has its unpleasant and – in the case of people potentially powerful like Sir Harry Wildair and Sir Fopling Flutter – its dangerous or hurtful side. To avoid fops being merely trivial, to avoid them fulfilling only their comic function within the play, this unpleasantness and this power must be seized upon and played through.

6 *The Critic's View*

MICHAEL BILLINGTON

Michael Billington *has been drama critic for* The Guardian *since 1971. He is a frequent contributor to American journals, including the* New York Times *and* Interview *magazine. He broadcasts regularly on BBC Radio for both* Critics' Forum *and* Kaleidoscope. *He is author of several theatre books including studies of Alan Ayckbourn and Tom Stoppard and, most recently, the first biography of Dame Peggy Ashcroft.*

How on earth did the British theatre manage without the Swan?

The short answer is that it didn't. Our knowledge of our non-Shakespearean heritage — particularly that period from 1570 to 1750 — has always depended on a handful of dedicated enthusiasts. Bernard Miles in the days of the old Puddle Dock Mermaid regularly revived lesser-known Elizabethan and Jacobean work: I recall a wonderful production of *The Shoemaker's Holiday* with John Woodvine as a ripely genial Simon Eyre. The Havergal-Prowse-Macdonald triumvirate who run the Glasgow Citizens have also enthusiastically explored the Jacobean-Caroline period delighting in the florid decadence of Webster and Ford. And the RSC itself over the years has dipped into the work of Shakespeare's contemporaries but, inevitably, in a rather fitful manner: as Trevor Nunn pointed out, it was something of a scandal that it had presented only three Ben Jonson plays in a quarter-century.

But, until the Swan arrived, revivals from the richest period of English drama were one-off affairs lacking permanence or continuity. *The Duchess of Malfi* and *The White Devil* have had a fair innings over the years largely because they provide showcase roles for star-actresses. *Volpone* and *The Alchemist* occasionally got done. Otherwise collectors of rare plays were rather like ornithologists ever ready to dash over the country, with binoculars trained, in quest of The Great Auk. I remember Nottingham Playhouse in its first season gave us Ian McKellen in *Sir Thomas More*, a vivid piece of Shakespeare Apocrypha and very moving in its portrait of noble martyrdom ('Point me the way, I ne'er was here before' cries the hero on his way to the block). Nottingham again, under Stuart Burge, gave us Jonson's *The Devil is an Ass* with its portrait of a minor devil at large in the world of London business ('You talk of a university. Why hell is a grammar school to this'). *The Changeling* has also enjoyed periodic revivals possibly because of its ironic interweaving of lust, loot and class. In general, however, our attitude towards classic English drama has always been one of the Lucky Dip with isolated directors raiding Santa's sackful to see what they could come up with.

It was Matthew Arnold, of course, who wrote 'The theatre is irresistible. Organise the theatre.' The good thing about the Swan is that it provides a permanent home for the exploration of the byways of English drama. It also offers a seductive and appropriate environment. 'A Jacobean Habitat' one colleague rather dismissively called it, but that seems to me its strength. It combines the shape and structure of a courtyard theatre with the comfort and conveniences of a modern building. I cannot share the pedagogic enthusiasm of those who want to re-construct Shakespeare's Globe since I have no great wish to stand in a light rain in the middle of the afternoon listening to Shakespeare's plays while jets roar by overhead. Neither, on the other hand, do I much enjoy sitting in some modern breezeblock civic monstrosity which has all the warmth and intimacy of a car-park. The best theatres I know are those that combine old and new. The Olivier. The Young Vic. And now the Swan which wraps the playgoers around the stage and which ensures everyone can see and hear without undue strain.

The Swan has, at a stroke, widened the English repertoire. But what effect has it had on the RSC? The popular argument, at the moment, is that theatrically more means worse: that by creating a new venue in Stratford, and seeking for a matching home in London, the RSC has over-extended itself, become too big for its own and everyone else's boots and somehow dissipated its quality. I am not sure I agree with any of this. It is certainly true that, during the Swan's first 1986 season, there was more excitement to be found there than in the Main House. It is also true that the experiment of using the Mermaid as a London base for the Swan repertory didn't really pay off. But quantity doesn't automatically mean a decline in quality. In 1987 the RSC staged fifteen productions in Stratford – five in each of its three houses – and the result, with actors of the calibre of Antony Sher, Brian Cox, Harriet Walter and Estelle Kohler around, was one of the strongest seasons in memory. A prodigious output is part of the RSC's policy. Is the Berliner Ensemble method of staging one or two new productions a year really to be preferred?

When it comes to the aesthetic impact of the Swan, the thing that I have noticed most is that it encourages an easy, outgoing style of performance. On the main Stratford stage, an actor addressing the house has to choose whether or not to pitch his remarks at stalls, circle or balcony. In the Swan, it seems much easier to acknowledge and embrace the whole. audience. Indeed the productions that have worked least well there have been those that seem to have been encased behind some invisible proscenium arch failing to take into account the theatre's opportunity for instant contact.

One can hardly blame Barry Kyle for not getting it right first time out but the production of his that christened the Swan, *The Two Noble Kinsmen*, here attributed to Shakespeare and Fletcher, seems in retrospect to have been rather enclosed. He steeped the work in Oriental ritual with Theseus as a red-robed Japanese war-lord plucking symbolic roses from his wife's bosom, and with Palamon and Arcite as a pair of kimono-clad Samurai uttering cries of 'Hi' and 'Ho' (it's off to work they go) before embarking on battle. The Japanese treatment of English classics makes sense when a production stems from Tokyo: in the West it is becoming a bit of a modish cliché. A British director working at the Folger Library's Theatre in Washington recently told me that he intended to give DC a Samurai version of *Richard II*: I was too polite to ask what on earth that had to do with mystical medieval notions of kingship and a belief in the sacred holiness of God's anointed.

But though Mr Kyle's production was lively and colourful and certainly removed any fears the Swan might turn into an academic plaything, it could actually have happened anywhere. It proved that the play might have been called *The Two Lovesick Women* rather than *The Two Noble Kinsmen* since the most interesting characters were Amanda Harris's warred-over Emilia and Imogen Stubbs's Gaoler's Daughter pursuing Palamon with portable bedding rather like the Crazy Gang's Charlie Naughton eagerly following a luscious sleepwalker with a mattress. But the production never really used the intimacy of the space. Bob Crowley's design, with its mixture of suspended platforms, pigtailed Athenians and banner-waving Cecil Sharp folksiness, was also rather cluttered and busy. The Swan is often at its best when at its simplest.

A lot, of course, depends on the play. Ben Jonson was a documentary realist and so Sue Blane's designs for *Every Man In His Humour* were rightly full of tables, tavern-bars, ladders for the City scenes while a signpost encrusted with pigeon-droppings suggested Moorfields. But the success of this production lay in John Caird's scrupulous affection for the text and in the way the actors played to the house. The most exciting performance came from Henry Goodman as the merchant Kitely, a paranoid bourgeois as obsessed with cuckoldry as Shakespeare's Ford. Hazlitt tells us that Kean's Kitely depended on 'the artifice of abrupt transitions'. So too did Mr Goodman's. His head jerked like that of a manic marionette, his body was subject to an endless series of internal volcanic eruptions and at one moment, while having a headache soothed by his wife, he hissed at us 'It's this new disease.' It was very funny. It was also based on something real. And for me Mr Caird set a new standard in modern Jonson productions by giving us characters seen from within rather than caricatures glimpsed from without. Mr Caird also achieved something relatively revolutionary in RSC terms by playing a period comedy in its original setting.

But Mr Caird clearly has a thing about Jonson and I feel should be allowed to work his way through the neglected canon. (How about *Epicoene*, *Sejanus*, *The Staple of News*?). In the winter of 1987 he gave us the first professional production, since a single disastrous performance in 1629, of Jonson's *The New Inn* and what an extraordinary play it turned out to be. It was rather like *The Tempest* translated to a Barnet pub with a whiskered fixer of a landlord declaring 'I imagine all the world's a play' and arranging a match between two of his guests: Lovel, a wracked melancholic, and Lady Frampul, a professional virgin. The inn is turned into a medieval Court of Love ruled over by Lady Frampul's chambermaid who decrees that Lovel give two hours service to her mistress and discourse on the nature of love.

I don't think I have ever seen the Swan better used, in that the setting and the theatre became as one. But the play also emerged as a neo-Shakespearean dream in which character was revealed through disguise, families were re-united and marital love was seen as a symbol of earthly harmony. It banished for ever the notion of Jonson as an over-erudite classicist sadly lacking in heart. Yet the play also contained elements of hilarious social comedy such as the sub-plot involving a kinky tailor who dresses his wife in his clients' clothes and then transports her from Romford to Hounslow pleasuring her the while: thus does the sexual fetishism of the suburbs make its debut in English drama.

The production played only a handful of performances at the tag-end of the season and never made it to London. But it was a model of how Jonson should be played: with vigour, wit and affection. For contrast, one only had to look at Richard Eyre's National Theatre revival of *Bartholomew Fair* which first of all transposed the action to Victorian London, which crowded the stage with fairground stalls leaving precious little room for the actors, which weakly had the gross, sweaty, earth-larding Pig-woman, Ursula, played by a man and which trivialised Jonson's exposé of religious hypocrisy by showing Zeal-Of-The-Land-Busy to be clad in pink, frilly, female underwear. I have no doubt Mr Eyre loves Jonson as much as Mr Caird. But the impression he left was that he didn't fully trust his author and felt that a smart metropolitan audience had to have the play re-packaged. But one virtue of the Swan, so far little noticed, is that it almost obliges a director to stick within the chosen conventions of the play's period; and I only hope, over the years, that it becomes a kind of unofficial Jonson Memorial Theatre.

The Swan also seems to bring out a quality of mellow humanism that, under Trevor Nunn's directorship, was one the RSC's trademarks. Nunn himself returned to Stratford, after too long a sojourn in the barren field of West End musicals, to direct a conflated version of Thomas Heywood's *The Fair Maid of the West* at the Swan at the end of its first season; and he, more than any director, showed what a versatile space it is. He not merely broke down the barriers by having the actors scattered around the auditorium ready for a chat and a drink before the play started. He had chases through the aisles, actors swinging across the stage on ropes and even muskets being fired into the Swan galleries in the course of a naval battle. Admittedly some of the devices seemed to be there to prop up a rather broken-backed play, but Nunn's production reminded us that the Swan has a great capacity to become whatever a director wishes it to be. Obviously it can turn into a tavern. But here the great piece of transforming magic came when ropes were tethered to the rails running round the stage, a couple of canvas-sheets became two sails and trestle-tables were arranged in step-formation to suggest multi-levelled decks. Instantly we were on board a ship; and for me this simple transformation, involving an act of imaginative participation on the part of the spectators, was infinitely more exciting than lavish displays of hi-tech design costing millions. (See page 59.)

Obviously as a performance-space the Swan is well-suited to comedy. What we have yet to see fully-tested is its suitability for tragedy. In the second season a number of darker plays were presented, including *The Jew of Malta* and *The Revenger's Tragedy*, but even these have their moments of dark laughter and depend upon a slightly conspiratorial relationship between the stage and the auditorium. To date, the only unrelieved tragedy we have been given is Shakespeare's *Titus Andronicus* and it proved how effective (given a director of Deborah Warner's talent) sobriety and austerity can be. They say *Titus* is a rare play: I have seen half a dozen productions including a startling one many years ago in the Bristol Old Vic with Simon Callow as Titus and with Adrian Noble as director filling the stage with rivers of blood. Ms Warner eschewed blood, thunder, rhetoric and decor and focused on acting and language. I found the experience profoundly moving. It became a play about grief rather than violence; about how much pain and torment the human mind can stand before it twists into madness. Instead of a blood-boltered shocker we had a genuinely neo-Senecan play about stoicism in the face of adversity. Given the success of *Titus*, I hope in years to come the Swan ventures further into the tragic repertoire. Surely

Every Man In His Humour
Ben Jonson
Sue Blane's costume sketches for Captain Bobadill (*Pete Postlethwaite*) and Master Matthew (*Philip Franks*).

Cptn. Bobadill
Pete Postlethwaite

Mr. Matthew
Phillip Franks

The Fair Maid of the West
Thomas Heywood
Set design for the inn at the opening of the
play: designer, John Napier.
PHOTOGRAPH: DONALD COOPER

The Fair Maid of the West
Thomas Heywood
Bess Bridges (*Imelda Staunton*) in a ship-board
skirmish.
PHOTOGRAPH: DONALD COOPER

Trundle

Peck

Jordan

Trevor Martin

Jimmy Gardner

Griff Jones

The New Inn
Ben Jonson
Sue Blane's costume drawings for Trundle
(*Trevor Martin*), Peck (*Jimmy Gardner*) and
Jordan (*Griffith Jones*).

it is time again for Shakespeare's *Timon*. And how about Massinger's *The Roman Actor*, Marston's *The Malcontent*, Ford's *Love's Sacrifice*, Rowe's *The Fair Penitent*?

The Restoration has, of course, been thoroughly examined in the recent 1988 season with comedies by Farquhar, Wycherley and Etherege. Comedies did I say? What struck me about the season was the underlying darkness of many of these plays with their emphasis on greed, untrammelled ego and hollow narcissism. For me much the most interesting of the productions was Garry Hynes's version of *The Man of Mode* which presented us with a world of decayed passion, masculine cruelty and mirror-gazing solitude. One scene sticks obstinately in my memory: a nocturnal encounter in Dorimant's lodgings when Sir Fopling Flutter (another of Simon Russell Beale's collection of unstrung *beaux*) gazes around in desperation for a mirror since, as he says, in a glass a man may entertain himself. 'Tis the best diversion in our retirements' he poignantly claims, summing up for me a whole world of terrifying masturbatory solitude. And you will have to look hard in Restoration Comedy to find a scene as rackingly harsh as that in which Dorimant finally discards his ageing mistress, Mrs Loveit. I used, in all honesty, to be wary of Restoration Comedy thinking it to be full of dandy-mincing, fan-waving and interchangeable raillery. One thing the Swan season has taught me is that each writer had his own style and that there is real emotional pain lurking underneath the theatrical artifice.

What then has the Swan achieved so far? Thirteen productions in three seasons with remarkably few duds. A growing awareness on the part of theatregoers that there is much more to the English repertoire than the hallowed band of eternally revived classics. An increasing confidence on the part of directors, designers and actors in the use of the space. An end to the smirking critical platitude that if a play hasn't been revived for 300 years there is usually a good reason for it. Perhaps, above all, a realisation that there is a communicable pleasure in seeing a play from a past era that may not be an out-and-out masterpiece but that still unlocks a piece of the past. We go to the theatre for many reasons. But surely one of them is to discover how people lived and thought and talked in other generations. We, after all, endlessly tour country houses and stately homes to learn what beds people slept in, what pictures they collected, what plates they ate off. Why should we not go to the theatre to learn of their conjugal relations, their manners of speech, their moral confusion? And, if the play is any good at all, we may also find a mirror held up to our own likeness. The possibilities for the Swan are enormous. I only hope that in years to come the RSC will continue to unearth more of the buried treasure of English drama.

Every Man In His Humour
Ben Jonson
Pete Postlethwaite as Bobadill (*right*) with
Ed Kno'well and his friends.
PHOTOGRAPH: JOE COCKS

Every Man In His Humour
Ben Jonson
Bobadill (*Pete Postlethwaite*) supervises a duel
from a chair.
PHOTOGRAPH: JOE COCKS

7 *The Director in the Swan*

TREVOR NUNN

I read *The Fair Maid of the West*, both parts, when I was at university and I've always had a perverse affection for it. Even at that stage I think I recognised that what I was reading was pretty much the Elizabethan equivalent of a television series. It's not pitched at a much higher level. It is 'jingoistic', and the issues that it raises it doesn't investigate. I mean it raises them in banner head-lines; it quotes issues but it doesn't deal with them. But the affection I had for it was because so much of the narrative of the work was unexpected and *entirely* opposite from the dramaturgical notions of the Elizabethan theatre we take to be general when we read Shakespeare. When you read *The Fair Maid of the West* and you also understand that it was an immensely popular work – you begin to think that perhaps Shakespeare's ideas *weren't* general.

My affection for *The Fair Maid* survived over many years, but I nevertheless recognised that its exuberant, careless dramaturgy required a particular kind of space if it were to work. To do such a play at The Other Place would, by definition, be at half cock, since it is outgoing, brash and boisterous. I suppose two years before the Swan opened I was saying at Planning meetings, 'There is a play called *The Fair Maid of the West* and I bag it.'

Fortunately, nobody else wanted to 'bag it'. I undertook to conflate (John Barton's word) the two parts. Though Part 2 is rather sparse, I thought it would be a great shame to do only Part 1, because some delightful incidents would be lost from the second play and there would also be several things we would want to cut from the more substantial Part 1 leaving it too short to make a full evening, and therefore conflation was the answer. Of course, it turned out to be something of a rewrite of which Heywood might approve. It must be said that since he gave his name to more than 200 plays, it is more than likely he approved of several re-writes during his lifetime, or that he was the re-writer of other people's texts. That must have been how it worked, and so I didn't have a sense of doing something sacrilegious. Heywood would have been quite party to the sort of paste-and-paper job that I was doing, I hope not unintelligently. And after all, we were doing it because having located the main themes, we wished to keep them going and expand on some of them. I think most of all, Heywood would have approved of a feeling of well-being and happiness and generosity that pervaded the evening. That was the feeling that we all had when rehearsing. We all agreed it would have been very unlikely that such a writer would not be a nice man.

Peter Brook once said to me, 'I hear that you're doing a production of *Romeo and Juliet* — well if you take my advice, you'll cut the text to about an hour and twenty minutes and have terrific fights.' I don't think he intended me to do that — and indeed I didn't — but I did remember the joke when I was approaching *The Fair Maid of the West*, and having counted up the number of fights and pitched battles in the story, I thought, if I *were* making a pirate adventure movie — how significant would the fights be? and why did Heywood put the fights there in the first place? He would have understood Hollywood's delight in violence that is amusing because it is freed from consequences. In *Fair Maid*, nobody gets hurt. And so the production was appropriately rumbustious and hilarious.

We had as enjoyable a time as I can remember in rehearsal — obviously the friendly Conference Hall exerting its old influence. There were a number of actual *friends* in the Company, like Joe Melia, Pete Postlethwaite and Paul Greenwood and I made a new friend in Imelda (Staunton). I had always wanted to work with her from the time of an audition encounter years ago for *Cats*. Early on I took the decision that if I cast somebody who appeared to reflect the hyperbolic descriptions that are given of Bess in the text, then an essential comic ingredient would disappear. There had to be a gap, a gulf, between the events and people being described and the folk doing the enactment, and what I wanted was 'a play performed.' I wanted somebody who'd have a comic distance between her and the role to make up and to play off.

I talked to Imelda about being a bar-maid who would then *play* a paragon. And a princess. Imelda needed no encouragement to create somebody with an aura, while at the same time being able to comment on it and play *with* the audience about the disparity between the role and herself. It was meat and drink to Imelda. I needed somebody who would instantly find her way into an audience's affections because of a sort of latent tenderness in her nature. I needed a clown. I needed a singer. The play is to some extent a sea-port saga — I mean a traveller's tale of the high seas — and required a pub performance, with a folk-song ingredient. I don't think any of the decisions that I made were startingly original or unexpected, but I do think that they were on the side of the play and that they released what was best in it.

By the same token, I was looking for an actor who would be able to exploit a comic distance between himself and the role of the King of Morocco. I had several black actors in the Company — and indeed I believe above all things in the development of integrated casting — particularly in Stratford and particularly when exploring Elizabethan texts. But the last thing I wanted was a black actor playing a bombastic, untrustworthy black potentate because all comic momentum would thereby disappear. Such casting would have required me to be extremely earnest and careful about all of the King of Fez incidents — whereas the incident that we *must* be serious about is the friendship that grows up between the young white sea-captain and the black Jaffa. That's a narrative strand that is fundamental to Heywood's intentions. It *must* be serious.

So I moved the casting round and, of course, to have Joe Melia was wonderful. It's not only that performances become entirely spontaneous, dangerous and hair-raising with Joe in the cast, but the *rehearsals* become so. Everybody has to take their lives into their hands when Joe is in the building, and that's a condition that I thrive on. I think that *The Fair Maid of the West* devoid of spontaneity and invention during performance on the night, with the audience, would have lost much of its energy and its almost pantomimic nature.

The production expressed everything I believed about the Swan when I talked about it being a public space. The show quite literally stormed the audience, surrounded them, took place amongst them and demanded from them an imaginative response.

The Fair Maid of The West
Thomas Heywood
Spencer (*Sean Bean*), Bess Bridges
(*Imelda Staunton*) and Captain Goodlack
(*Paul Greenwood*).
PHOTOGRAPH: MICHAEL LE POER TRENCH

JOHN CAIRD

There are enormous advantages to working in the Swan. First and foremost it's a very warm place to be, familiar. It makes the production of comedy much easier in that you can share it with an audience rather than *demonstrate* it to an audience. In tragic work, you can get to the raw nerve ends of people's imagination in the same way that, in comic work, you can get to their funny bones. However, it's not like The Other Place, it isn't primarily an actor's space, because the stage is not just the focal point of the audience's attention, it is also a public platform.

It's a difficult space to direct in, because there seems to be at one end of the acting space the likeness of a large proscenium arch, but you can't use the space as if it was a Victorian scenic frame as in the Main House at Stratford, or in any theatre built on Victorian principles. If you do try to put pictures in it which are in any way two-dimensional, only a small proportion of the audience is going to see them as the designer and director intend them to be seen, head-on. Over half the audience are going to have either a limited view, or no view at all. There's nothing more disunifying in theatre than showing pictures on the stage which can't be simultaneously appreciated by all the audience.

Michael Reardon, the architect of the Swan, said something very illuminating about the three spaces at Stratford. The Main House is an audience space: the whole building is dominated by the audience, and it's a place where the audience matters as much as what's happening on stage. The Swan, as he puts it, is an author's space, it's a place where the play stands up. The Other Place is an actor's space where, by the very nature of its lay-out, the actor generates the excitement, and the audience experiences a sense of voyeurism. Joe Melia has said that the Swan is a cabaret space.

There are some slight technical problems with the Swan which if we'd been aware of we would perhaps have been more careful about, in the design stage. There is no way of exiting downstage so that you disappear from the audience's view without breaking one or other of the conventions that the performance has worked hard to set up. For instance, if you exit downstage right, there are three possibilities. You can go through the audience and turn left and you end up in a little stairwell from which you cannot retreat, and from where you must eventually reappear; if you do break out of this little prison you have to crash through some exit doors into the night outside. If you go straight ahead, you go through the main entrance doors and let in all that bright foyer light, reminding an audience that it's a public space and not to do with the world you're creating on stage. Or you turn right and end up almost going back onto the stage you've just left. If you exit downstage *left*, the only way out of view of the audience is into a concrete corridor and up three flights of stairs, through the dressing rooms of the Main House.

John Caird *has been Associate Director of the RSC since 1977. He has directed over twenty productions for the Company (both in Stratford and in London) including* Les Miserables *and* Nicholas Nickleby *(both with Trevor Nunn). For the RSC at the Swan he has directed two plays by Ben Jonson –* Every Man In His Humour *(opened 15 May 1986) and* The New Inn *(opened 4 November 1987).*

A very difficult thing for directors to conquer in the Swan is the problem of spatial relationships. Because the stage is a long tongue poking out into the audience, surrounded on three sides, the prime acting space is right down on the tip of the tongue. It's a trap to try to play upstage so that all the audience can see the speaker's face, at all times, because you end up playing *everything* right up there, miles away. However, if you do come down to the centre – the focused actor has to have somebody to speak to downstage, and any actor sitting downstage of the focused actor and behaving as interlocutor automatically masks the focused actor from somebody in the audience. The problem requires completely new techniques of direction.

I'm quite certain that Jonson's plays have never worked and never will work in large proscenium arch theatres. They need an audience's close proximity, because practically everything that Jonson wrote relies on recognition, and for an audience that means recognition of the finest details of human behaviour. Jonson is most criticised, I think unfairly, for not being like Shakespeare; for not presenting stories which require the characters to have their lives changed and to end the play different from, if not better than, when they started. This is, I suppose, one of the most obvious signatures – flavours – of Shakespeare's work. But for Jonson these notions of drama were preposterous. He saw the world as a place where people don't change except as a result of a life-long process. Jonson believed that theatre should pertain to reality in a precise way: for example it would not be natural for sometimes shy, undemonstrative, untheatrical people to project, or even know how to describe, their emotions on stage. This criticism, which Jonson has fallen most prey to, arises almost entirely from a critical community who are so steeped in Shakespeare that they can't hear another tone of voice. It's as if you've been listening to Mozart all your life and nothing else, and then you're played Beethoven. You'd find it bombastic.

Marlowe has fared badly in the Swan, exposed as a man with very little to say. At the end of *The Jew of Malta* I thought I had spent the evening in the presence of a deeply unpleasant man, a man I would turn down a dinner invitation from. However, I don't think I would have had that impression if I'd been sitting in a big 1500 seat theatre watching the epic sweep of one of his plays. The opposite is true of Jonson. If you play Jonson in a big theatre, you get the feeling that he's trivial, because the size of the building itself seems to reduce what he's trying to say. In a small space, you get the feeling of a man of deep, sympathetic, liberal human emotions who, although irritable, is extremely generous. You certainly get the feeling of a man with whom it would be fascinating to spend an evening.

The idea of people defined by one 'humour' within them is exploded on every page that Jonson ever wrote. All it needs is one intelligent look at one slice of dialogue, chosen at random in any one of his plays. Every page is packed full of complexity and ambiguity and ironic comment. What one has to do both as an academic and as a professional practitioner, is to surmise why Jonson felt it necessary to describe his work in terms of 'humours'. Just like Brecht's alienation theory, it was a reaction against theatrical tradition. Jonson was trying to validate and justify his work to an audience who were not used to watching slice-of-life drama.

Given all the busy-ness of a Jonson play, with all the storylines converging and separating, all the props, all the characters, directing Jonson is a real challenge. All the dramaturgical evidence is somewhere there in the text, but you really have to look for it. He doesn't spell it out. Some scenes are particularly difficult to stage because of the way that plots collide with each other. The really hard scene to direct in *Every Man* – there's only one absolutely stiff, stinkingly difficult scene – is the final one. Getting everybody into the right position on the stage is almost impossibly complicated.

Many years ago, I read all of Jonson's plays. I couldn't believe that a man who wrote *The Alchemist, Bartholomew Fair, Volpone* could, as I was being told, have written such a lot of garbage for the rest of his life. It just seemed to be nonsense. So I read the lot and I was utterly bowled over. I didn't read a bad play. Perhaps *Every Man Out of His Humour* wasn't terribly good. But I read ten plays that have never been done, like *The Staple of News*, a wonderful play, and *The Tale of a Tub*, a fantastically funny social comedy. *The New Inn* and *Every Man in His Humour* were the two plays that stood out for me more than any other. *Every Man In His Humour* seemed to have such fantastic raw energy. It was a play written by a man who was so full of himself, so completely bumptious about the state of the arts, that he felt he just had to write the best play of the 1590's. I felt he'd got very close to doing so. The other play which seemed just begging to be done was *The New Inn*. I longed to do it from the first moment I read it.

I think the real problem about *The New Inn* is the apparently unreconcilable schism between the serious scenes and the comic scenes. It is particularly difficult because Jonson's main comic butt, the satirisation of the ludicrous Spanish Grandee's behaviour, now seems terribly abstruse. I came to believe on rehearsing this that it must have been terribly abstruse even when he wrote it – perhaps deliberately so. In the comic scenes, he wan't trying to write broad burlesque, he was trying to observe as accurately as he could, the real underworld of *The New Inn* in a revolutionary way, and without authorial comment – almost like a Pinter play.

In *The New Inn* Jonson is often writing quite subjectively. In *Every Man In His Humour* on the other hand he is not present in any of the characters to any great extent, with the possible exception of young Edward Kno'well. I developed this character further than is clear in the text by making it an obvious portrait of the young Ben Jonson. This was achieved by casting Simon Russell Beale rather than Jeremy Irons, and by reinstating the marvellous speech about Poetry in the final scene – an obviously subjective authorial statement.

The character of young Edward stands out as the one Achilles' heel in the play, that Jonson hadn't been able to build up and protect – it's charming – not exactly a flaw – but a charming signature. *The New Inn* is much more personal than the rest of his plays, it's really Jonson's *Tempest*. I think there's no question at all that *The New Inn* was written in response to Jonson reading the first folio of Shakespeare's plays. For him to have read his friend's great canon of work must have filled him with all sorts of contradictory feelings. Because he was such a brilliant analyst of other people's work, he must have seen

Every Man In His Humour
Ben Jonson
Captain Bobadill (*Pete Postlethwaite*) teaches
Master Matthew (*Philip Franks*) the points of
self-defence.
PHOTOGRAPH: JOE COCKS

immediately the drift in Shakespeare from the early plays to *The Tempest*, the way he became more and more able to speak from the heart about his own feelings, while consistently disguising them in his characters, and the increasing sense of wisdom and serenity in the late plays. I'm sure it was Shakespeare's last works that decided Jonson to write a play about his own art, about how he worked and what he believed in. Shakespeare chose an island a long way from civilisation, a wild place, savage and forbidding. Prospero's imagination and inspiration are gleaned from the island. He is constantly being pulled back down into the mud by baser instincts, and still finds a way of making rough magic with the rawest of materials. Jonson's island is a suburban pub; you don't go any further from London than Barnet — just far enough away from your town house that you don't behave quite like you do at home. A man can get away from his aristocratic roots by becoming a gypsy, another can get away from his own natural suburban personality by dressing as a Spaniard — but no further than that. Jonson is saying, 'I only need a handful of people living in, or visiting, a pub to be able to explain what it is I feel about the whole world.'

For some time you think of the Host as the Prospero figure, and so he is up to a point. But then you realise that Lovel is Prospero. He is the calm that's at the centre, although he appears to be as much distressed as everybody else. As soon as he's given licence to speak, or as soon as Jonson has written the plot which allows him licence to speak, author and character select from the world's serious, philosophical values only two qualities, love and valour. Love, that makes a man lose himself and become mutable, and gives him his experience and his humanity. And Valour, which is what returns a man to himself — a man or a woman, Jonson doesn't make a distinction — in spite of experience, which might drive him to become vicious, but which instead enables him to cope with the world, and the vicissitudes within it. For a man like Jonson, who at the end of his life was suffering from such constant pain, a man who all his life had suffered so horribly from losses and despair, these two qualities, Love and Valour were paramount virtues. The Host is the practical Jonson, the master of ceremonies, the man who's done it all and who has a slightly shaky past. That's Jonson too. But the philosophical side of Jonson is centred in the character of Lovel.

We did a lot of research for both Jonson productions. I gave the actors research projects on the period, somewhat artificially divided up into subjects — the politics of the time, the foreign policy, the state of the army, medicine and medical knowledge, astronomy, theology, the state of scientific discovery and of travel, what were people eating, drinking, wearing, how were they swearing, fighting, what were the modes of courtly behaviour, what was the class system, what was the world of the servant like, or the constable? Each actor would go away with a research project and come back a week later with a ten minute dissertation on it. Some actors became absolute experts and treated us to forty minutes, or an hour and forty minutes. Others presented only a thumb-nail sketch of their subject. We ended up with a pretty complete world picture of the time which was an education for everybody including myself. The reason it's so successful as a way of looking at a socially realistic play is that it gives the whole company a view of the behaviour of the times which eventually becomes quite instinctive to them. A director doesn't stop people in rehearsal

The New Inn
Ben Jonson
Pru (*Deborah Findlay*) presides over the Court of Love, watched by Lady Frampul (*Fiona Shaw; standing, right*).

every few minutes and say, 'No, you wouldn't have done that' or 'No, you wouldn't have said that', because all the actors have learned for themselves what their world would have been like.

We ended the performance with a madrigal called 'In Going To My Naked Bed' by Richard Edwards. It's a madrigal I've always known. I've actually sung it as a boy at school! My brother has a collection of madrigals, and he found it for me. I'd remembered it from then. It's not a great piece of Elizabethan contrapuntal writing. It's a very simple fable about love. The positive power of love. The reason for choosing it was that for the first time in many years I found myself doing a play without any music in it at all. *Every Man In His Humour* doesn't have music, no songs, no ditties, nothing. It's also a play that would be killed stone dead if you had a scene-change lasting for more than a second. So you can't have music in the scene-changes. I therefore broke with RSC tradition and said that there wouldn't be any music at all throughout the production. However I also felt that there was something rushed about the way that Jonson ties up all the themes at the end, especially in the later, Folio version of the play. I went back to the Quarto a lot, to fill it out, to give the characters their proper moments of resolution. And I thought that after all the reconciliations it would be wonderful, magical, if we flooded the theatre with harmony, suddenly making the audience *aware* that they'd heard no music all evening.

My authority for that particular madrigal was not important; although it is certainly true that part singing was a great pastime of that period. Had I been making the film of *Every Man In His Humour* the credits would be coming up and I'd be taking a long shot at it all instead. The madrigal idea was actually borrowed from *The New Inn*, where it is a much more integral device. In their very different ways the singing of a madrigal at the end of both evenings proved to be a most satisfying and theatrical conclusion, for audience and ensemble alike.

BARRY KYLE

Barry Kyle *is an Associate Director of the RSC. He has directed almost thirty plays for the Company including Shakespeare and Fletcher's* The Two Noble Kinsmen *(opening production), Marlowe's* The Jew of Malta *(7 July 1987) and James Shirley's* Hyde Park *(7 April 1987) in the Swan. For the 1987 season he was Artistic Director with responsibility for the Swan.*

My first memory of the Swan theatre was standing in a hole filled with builders' rubble, just before Christmas 1984, with James Sargant explaining to me where the stage was. Bob Crowley and I had to design *The Two Noble Kinsmen* in the builders' rubble. Clearly, there were two different problems. One was, reviving *The Two Noble Kinsmen* is a fairly major and difficult operation in itself. Secondly, opening a new theatre is a difficult operation. We found with that first production that it was only when it came to London that it was reviewed properly as a production – on the whole the Swan theatre itself was reviewed when the production opened in Stratford. We followed, I would say, rather closely the prevailing orthodoxy about the building which existed before it opened: which was that the simplicity of the scenic arrangement should dictate the way in which the plays were done. What I mean by that is that the theatre has no wings – and at that stage it didn't really have a proper trap-door arrangement – it does now through the ingenuity of Geoff Locker who managed, without a budget, to smuggle a lift arrangement into the trap that the Swan provides for scene changes and for storage. But when we opened it was necessary to reveal the building itself and I remember that we reacted with horror if someone proposed hanging a lantern off the front surface of Michael Reardon's design. So the design thinking for the production was based very much on the idea that we should interfere with the space as little as possible.

I remember, very vividly, my first impression of the new building was its height – that what was most dynamic was the space above the stage. We tried to use that in *The Two Noble Kinsmen*, and I've tried to use it ever since in everything I've done in the Swan. I remember feeling that whenever you lifted the action up, it was going to be at the moment when the actor was about eight or nine feet above the level of the stage – that was the democratic point of the theatre. And when Gerard Murphy and Hugh Quarshie sat in the hanging cage that we designed for the prison in *The Two Noble Kinsmen*, or when John Carlisle delivered the Machevil speech from that position in *The Jew of Malta*, one had a sense that that was the point of command. There is still more potential in that at the Swan: the space has a sort of vertical life which is amazing. For *Hyde Park*, we wanted to create a sense of space – which you have to in a play about a park. When you are on a platform stage, the only way you can expand it is upwards. So we tried to create the sense almost of a mock proscenium arch. And we had two scenic pieces on the sides of the stage, which had mirrors on them. These were really more a response to the space than anything else. It was an attempt as it were to see the Park through the living room, out through the window. I think that particular idea turned out to be rather theoretical ultimately, but that was the thinking.

In *The Two Noble Kinsmen* we were always interested in the movement of things through the space, not in locking the space up with scenery. We had the idea that Hippolyta's wedding dress should be the set in the first scene. (See page 91.) In my view, *The Two Noble*

Kinsmen is a heterogeneous play, not a homogeneous play. It shows evidence of more than one hand. As such it is extremely difficult and, in my view, wrong, to attempt to unify it sylistically. The relationship between the Theban story and the sub-plot, which is the most difficult relationship, was one which did not need to be all put in the same idiom, the same culture. Everyone doing that play will come up against the issue of how you dramatise a world which is based on that kind of honour, that kind of chivalry. I remember the specific occasion when the design concept arose in rehearsal. We were playing around with the morris, and trying to find a link between the dancing and the fighting. When we worked on dance for the morris, and used the morris staves, it suddenly became obvious that, in some way, the fighting needed to involve staves as well, and *that* led to kendo. Kendo led to the eastern setting. We avoided making the countrymen rustic; they had a somewhat ceremonial appearance. (See page 79.) I would describe the reaction to the setting of the show as rather conservative. When the Swan opened, people wanted a completely pure experience – they didn't want a production which altered period and culture. By the time I did *Hyde Park* a year later, and moved the setting forward – about 250 years forward – there was absolutely no problem. When theatres open, particularly those with openly declared policies, there's a resistance towards putting the improvisation before the theme. For the opening of the Swan probably an absolutely flat-out Elizabethan production is politically what ought to have happened. But that's not the production that I would have wanted to do. . . .

I have been baffled by some of the press comments that have gone on about the good effect of the Swan starting to wear off, and the remarks about it being designed at Heals and Habitat, and that its spiritual home is NW3. I think that's complete rubbish. It's a question of the way in which the space is *used*. You can *misuse* the space, and you can engender that reaction. You can't ignore the Swan auditorium. In The Other Place you actually can; in the Swan you ignore the auditorium at your peril. You do a play in there and a play has its own needs and requirements, but the *theatre's* requirements are very loud, and you can't tone it down. I rejoice in that. In my view the Swan is the best new theatre I have ever sat in in my lifetime. It was a sensational achievement by Michael Reardon and as time goes by it will become more and more so. I can't think of any theatre that I enjoy directing in more.

The political meaning of the Swan is for me that it is a community theatre. The political context of the Barbican has often damaged us. It's not just what's *in* the building but actually what's outside the building. If you turn down a side-street in Islington to go to the Almeida, and park your car outside a house – and if outside the front door of the theatre there's someone trying to put their children to bed – through their windows you can see them doing it – that's completely different from a theatre which is on an island, or in a business district. One of the reasons The Other Place has been so important to the Royal Shakespeare Company is because it's *not* a theatre, it wasn't built as a theatre, it's got grass outside and people living around it. That is what I mean about the politics of a building, what it implies about the theatrical relationship with the community. For me the Swan relates directly to the community and not only because of its history as the Conference Hall. There was a community meaning to that space that has been kept.

The thing that I'm most proud of in the work that I have done at the Swan is that *Hyde Park* – a completely unknown play by James Shirley, that had never had a London revival – took a quarter of a million pounds at the box office in the Swan in that year. Because it was so difficult when we started it, I wouldn't let the actors do a read-through for two weeks, out of the fear that they would get so depressed. But we worked on it and we worked on it, and audiences found it extremely easy and very approachable. In some of the drama of that period, directors have to take a slightly more authorial attitude to their work and actually direct the vision of the piece, rather than directing it down to the last full-stop.

I wouldn't say that about Marlowe. As far as designing *The Jew of Malta* was concerned, I remember one of the first things we sat down and tried to work out was how to drop Barabas to his death. The first thing we designed was the dustbin that held all of Barabas's gold. The original intention was that he should die in the dustbin. The idea was that it would be brought back, be filled with oil, and burn. The thing that he collected his money in, he would die in. We were going to do it, but Alun (Armstrong), who I have to say is the physically bravest actor I've worked with, took one look and said he didn't feel he could do it. Obviously, when Alun dropped, if the drop was wrong, he would have killed himself. We could not solve this. The theatre technology was too unsophisticated, so the idea had to be altered. You must not have the wrong kind of technical ambition in the Swan.

The idea of doubling Machevil with Ferneze was in our minds from the beginning. It was almost the first idea I had. It was a casting idea, and casting ideas usually are the first ideas you have. I read *The Jew of Malta* when I was a student and thought it was unrevivable. I find the whole issue of anti-semitic drama and whether you should revive it very difficult. I've actually directed *The Merchant of Venice* in Israel, so I've been through this discussion at some length. It was quite influential on the thinking I had in *The Jew of Malta*. I couldn't bear the idea of it seeming to be an anti-semitic piece of work. *The Jew of Malta* is actually less anti-semitic than *The Merchant of Venice*. Its disgust is so comical, that it strips the world of tragic dignity. In some ways my production was too comic and too pastiche. Alun Armstrong and I felt it wasn't anti-Jew, it was anti-Arab, it was anti-Christian, it was anti-God – and that what we had to produce was a piece of black vitality on the stage. It was necessary to make Machevil connect with the other side. I didn't want to relate him only to Barabas. He does, after all, talk about Barabas somewhat contemptuously in the first speech. And we all thought that Barabas's failure in the fifth act was that he failed to be sufficiently Machiavellian. What happens is that he is killed by an act of trust and in that world the only way to survive is to be totally without scruples to the end.

Ever since the Swan opened, all the directors have been saying that it's the best Chekhov space in Europe. We came rather close to doing an extra production at the Swan this year of *The Seagull*. I, along with everybody else, would be interested in doing either Brecht or Chekhov in that theatre. But the question is should the policy change? I would say that amongst the RSC directors I am the hard-liner on this issue. I believe that at no point in theatre history has a theatre been opened specifically to look at that gold-mine of the seventeenth-century repertoire, which I believe is a national treasure. If we hand that away it will never come back again. I have been, and will continue to be, vocal and aggressive on this subject, because I think it really important. For example, to go on doing Jonson, all of Jonson, the plays by Jonson that no-one has heard of. I remember seeing *Epicoene* when I was a student, and it was like a voyage of discovery. When we get round to *The Staple of News* and *The Magnetic Lady* I would think that that would be equivalent. It would be incredibly important for the RSC to do that. The Swan is almost too attractive. Everyone's imagination is teeming with what you could do in there, and it's going to be a battle to hang on to its original repertoire. I believe we must.

DI TREVIS

Di Trevis *has worked, as both actress and director, for, among others, the Glasgow Citizens Theatre and the National Theatre Company. She was assistant director on* A New Way to Pay Old Debts *for the RSC at The Other Place. In 1987 she directed* The Revenger's Tragedy, *which opened at the Swan on 2 September. The production was designed by Michael Levine.*

I would like to say that first of all I was very excited at working at the Swan because just from visiting it, really even before it was finished when I was shown round in a tin hat, I could see that it was going to free a great deal in the actors. I felt that the terrible push to be heard that you have in the Main House wasn't going to be quite so troublesome for actors and that the shape of the theatre would engender a real creative excitement in the actor because the audience are so near. I thought that the space would be particularly interesting for the kind of play that *The Revenger's Tragedy* seemed to be. I felt it was going to belong to the genre of chamber horror so that in this enclosed space you could create a rather claustrophobic atmosphere, not only because of the subject matter of the play but also the wonderful language. So I was tremendously excited about working in the space. I then went earlier in the season to see a production and I began to see that there were immense problems as a director in staging on that stage. In a play like *The Revenger's Tragedy*, you start off fine because you've got Antony Sher on his own, you know that he can use the space as he wishes, but when you get that dreadful scene when the entire Court come on and the Duke and Duchess are found in bed and then there's the little scene between Spurio and his two servants which has to take place somewhere else, you've got so many bodies on the stage, and you can't pile them all against the back wall. Therefore you do have scenes where it's very problematic.

So what I decided was that we would in some way have to raise the back of the stage, because I felt that if a character was here and addressing people around him, I would be freer. Like most solutions, the solution that we came up with provided us with lots of problems. I used an upturned table, a sort of collapsed table. I really used the whole theatre, I had people running round the gangways. I suppose people thought this a hangover from the sixties, but actually it was an absolute necessity because I couldn't think how to get the sense of panic in any other way. I think the demands of *The Revenger's Tragedy* were enormous as far as staging was concerned. I am thinking for example of the trial scene near the beginning where you have to have such shifts of focus. I had the stage filled with quite an enormous number of people quite a lot of time.

My designer, Michael Levine, and I came up against all sorts of problems in designing a set. In the end I just said that I don't think in a place like the Swan you change anything, you have a single set, because especially *The Revenger's Tragedy* has to go at a terrific pace. The plays are so interesting at this time, it's like they're writing for film. They're not limited at all by the limits of the theatre, they just take you on these fantastically swift-changing scenes. I was very determined that we should keep that.

I'd just been, before I started *The Revenger's Tragedy*, in Central America, in El Salvador, where there's the most dreadful war going on, and people are either rich or completely destitute, and I felt that this terribly decadent world of *The Revenger's Tragedy* was rather like that. We came up with the idea that if people had lost wealth in a society like this they were suddenly living hand-to-mouth, in whatever place they could find. You don't have to go to El Salvador to find people living in cardboard boxes but that's the sort of image that we had. Therefore we came up with the idea that people really lived like vermin, under tables, in holes in the ground, in complete poverty. I was also very keen to use the height of the Swan, the three storeys. I used the hole in the ground because I thought of the idea that you were in this palace that went on down into the ground and up into the air. So we constructed a high level too so that behind the gauze curtain people would go up to upper chambers, a sort of dense warren.

That's really where the idea for the costume designs came from. I said to Michael that I would love to get the sense of the magnificence, the seeming magnificence of the Court, especially in the opening images. I felt that it would be marvellous if we could see the Court, how incredible they looked, how luxurious and rich, and then as we got closer realise how the whole thing was completely decayed. Because only a society in the worst condition of decay could really stoop to this kind of violence and brutality and animal ambition. You saw a magnificent costume and then as the person came nearer you, or the lights went up, you realised that it was in tatters. What looked like make-up was actually pustules on the skin, filth.

I have to say that I enjoyed very much doing *The Revenger's Tragedy*, but the look and the feel of the Swan isn't aesthetically up my street. There are many many good things about it and I'm very pleased that we have this house, but I do sometimes feel that I just need a couple of hooks and then I can hang some cups up in all that wood. All that wood is very difficult to transform but I'm sure that's because what was intended was that nothing but the word should transform the stage. I think that was absolutely the intention, which I didn't quite fulfil. People say that it's an extremely elaborate visual production but it's not. The set is absolutely simple.

I always work through movement in everything I do, because I see too much work that is really people trying to inhabit another century, but stepping physically straight from the twentieth century, so that to all intents and purposes their bodies are in blue jeans. The world of *The Revenger's Tragedy* is a world where at any moment you might have a dagger in your back, where you have to have eyes that can see round corners and into shadows and you have a whole body language that is about private messages being passed, non-verbally. You have the incredible physical energy of oppression and locked-in ambition and tension, and of course it has to be the character's tension, not the actor's tension. The actors have to be completely free.

I felt that the manners of the Court needed a lot of attention. We did a lot of work through body language on hierarchy. I've always worked through dance, the dance of the period. I think that helps enormously. Just to hear the music of the period itself helps actors imaginatively construct their work. The pavanne is an extremely difficult dance to do well. Jane (Gibson) did a marvellous thing. Very early in rehearsal she said to one of the

The Two Noble Kinsmen
Shakespeare and Fletcher
The Gaoler's Daughter (*Imogen Stubbs*) and
Morris dancers watched by Hippolyta (*left:
Anna Nygh*) and Emilia (*right: Amanda Harris*).
PHOTOGRAPH: DONALD COOPER

The Jew of Malta
Christopher Marlowe
The death of Barabas (*Alun Armstrong*),
photographed after Barbican transfer by
Donald Cooper.

The Revenger's Tragedy
Cyril Tourneur
The ducal family.
Designed by Michael Levine.
PHOTOGRAPH: DONALD COOPER

The Revenger's Tragedy
Cyril Tourneur
The Duchess, centre (*Julie Legrand*) with her
sons, Supervacuo (*Mike Dowling*) and
Ambitioso (*Jim Hooper*).
PHOTOGRAPH: JOE COCKS

younger actors, 'Don't make a mistake'. He looked outraged. 'Don't make a mistake, you're in a world where people don't make mistakes, and if you do make a mistake nothing in your body or your face must indicate that you have.' We had dancing competitions where people danced for their lives. And that was what really provided us with the opening image. I knew that the death-filled dance at the end with the masks would provide a climax, and I felt that we should be prepared for that, we should be in a world where this kind of event occurred. A kind of antitype of the normal Elizabethan world where the idea of the dance represented social harmony, and the order of the universe. It's a world of privilege turning fearsome and vindictive and violent. There's something so sombre and really terrible about that world. I think of all the dances the pavanne requires such a slow and held control. I think that that's what is so immensely difficult about it and also gives it this undertug of intrigue, because the upper body doesn't move, but you're aware all the time of moving with other people, and having to keep in columns and lines.

It is a very tense play. People are enclosed in small spaces, doing things that they think are private, and they never are private. I didn't have any non-speaking actors in my production and I told the courtiers throughout rehearsals, having explained the set, that they should feel that they could as it were loiter, linger, spy and appear at the tops of ladders, peeping round. I also had many years before seen a marvellous film about a court and power — Rosellini's film about Louis XIV — where I was very struck by the scene in the early morning where the King was sleeping and the servants slept on the floors. Then as I was doing *The Revenger's Tragedy* I read a book on Saudi Arabia about body servants for each young prince. So I wanted an effect where at any moment somebody would only have to lift a finger and a servant would be there. We did a lot of exercises about trying to pass messages without speaking. We did a lot of work with the servants and the masters and mistresses, where the servants had to guess what the master wanted without anything being said.

When I was thinking about talking to you on my way here today I felt I ought to say that whatever I've said as a director I know that actors love working in the Swan. Designers and directors find the personality of the Swan quite strong and they sometimes have to work against it. It's all that wood somehow, and it's all very wholesome and it's all very clean. . . . I like the confines of the space, as it were, the parameters of the space to disappear when you're watching a piece of theatre. That doesn't happen in the Swan.

Stage set for *The Jew of Malta*
Christopher Marlowe
Designer: Bob Crowley.
PHOTOGRAPH: GEOFF LOCKER

8 Designing for the Swan

BOB CROWLEY

Bob Crowley *has designed for a wide range of theatres and opera companies including Bristol Old Vic, The Royal Exchange, The National Theatre, The Welsh National Opera, Kent Opera, and the Royal Opera House. His work for the RSC has included designs for* The Irish Play, Thirteenth Night, The Forest, The Taming of the Shrew, King Lear, Measure for Measure, The Time of Your Life, A New Way to Pay Old Debts, Henry V, Love's Labour's Lost, As You Like It, Les Liaisons Dangereuses, Flight, Principia Scriptoriae *and* Macbeth. *He has designed* The Two Noble Kinsmen *and* The Jew of Malta *for the Swan.*

I've designed two productions for the Swan, the very opening show – *The Two Noble Kinsmen* – and *The Jew of Malta*. The first one was really designing the show without getting to grips with the theatre. There wasn't a theatre until the last day. The guts of it were there, but one had no experience of it, so I don't think that's really representative of working in the Swan. My experience of doing *The Jew of Malta* there was an extremely pleasant one. It actually worked terribly well for the play, and released the play in lots of ways. But I'm not sure it's a designer's theatre. I'm not really convinced that the Swan offers the same opportunities as most theatres I know of that size. The problem I have with it as a designer is that it imposes itself, hugely, and no matter what you do, you design against it, at your peril. Unlike The Other Place, which constantly changes its character, there's something about the Swan that can't yield.

I think it's something to do with the raised platform. There's something about smaller theatres where the audience actually traverse the stage when they walk into it, like the Young Vic or The Other Place. I remember when we were working on *The Two Noble Kinsmen* we did consider working on the floor, so that the audience shared the same floor with the actors. That didn't happen, because of the sight lines. It would be nice to think you could take that stage out and get that actor-to-audience relationship back, and solve the sightline problems in another way. It seems to me the priorities are the wrong way round.

The height of the Swan is, again, a problem. It's wonderful having height over an actor's head. I *used* it in *The Two Noble Kinsmen* and in *The Jew of Malta*, although I think it was more successful with the *Jew*. I mean one had that facility. Not every play demands it and not every actor or designer would want to use it, but if you don't you feel you're neglecting a whole area of that stage. Height is therefore very important, and needs to be tackled, constantly.

My design for *The Jew of Malta* I tried to make complementary to the space, in the sense that I used the wood, and the colours, and so on, but it worries me that one would find it quite difficult to do something cold there. A play that has to do with poverty would be quite difficult to do. It's difficult to do in places like the Barbican as well, but somehow all the gains you make when working in a small space are slightly compromised by, in particular, the way the building has been finished. It may be it just needs to be aged, and weathered, and used a bit. It sounds a pretentious thing to do, but somehow if one could take back that very stripped-pine look of the place, in terms of colour and texture, and rough it up a little. It's still a new theatre, so all these things can be solved.

Sometimes I have the impression the audience feels slightly removed from what's going on up there on the stage, they're not quite part of it. Even with entrances through the auditorium, I always feel the actors are coming in through the *Swan*. I think it has something to do with that platform stage. In some plays it's absolutely fine that the actors should be remote from and indeed dominate the audience.

Theatres, and specifically the Swan, have sometimes been described as creating 'sacred spaces'. I think if one wants to create a sacred space that's up to directors, designers and actors together to create that feeling. If an architect has created that feeling to begin with, it just limits your scope and the possibilities of doing other forms of theatre. And somehow when I think of the Swan in the past three years, the *theatre* is what I remember most. Some fantastic work has been done there, but I always come away with this image of the Swan overriding the memory of the production.

The Two Noble Kinsmen
Shakespeare and Fletcher
Arcite (*Hugh Quarshie*).
PHOTOGRAPH: DONALD COOPER

SUE BLANE

Sue Blane *trained at the Central School of Art and Design. She has designed for theatre (including* The Glasgow Citizens Theatre, Manchester Royal Exchange *and* The Royal Court*), opera (Scottish Opera, Welsh National Opera and The English National Opera at the Coliseum), films (including* The Rocky Horror Picture Show, Lady Jane *and* Absolute Beginners*). Her recent work for the RSC includes* A Question of Geography *(at The Other Place) as well as* Every Man In His Humour *and* The New Inn *at the Swan.* Every Man in His Humour *opened on 15th May 1986,* The New Inn *on 4th November 1987.*

When I did my design for *Every Man In*, we were very aware that the theatre was as new as a new set, so that there seemed very little reason to come up with a design concept, as you would have to on the Main Stage, or, indeed, in any proscenium theatre. It was quite clear that the theatre was going to give us the atmosphere – perfect for Jonson – which, indeed, it did. What we needed to find was a means of getting from one scene to another. This was particularly important with Jonson.

What John (Caird) was doing, quite rightly, was domesticating it – so it needed all the furniture and the props, it needed the sign-posts of real life. I have no idea where the notion of hanging up all the props came from. All I remember really is having a lot of fun with a model of the Swan Theatre. I spent hours hanging things up on bits of card and making little pulleys. Luckily, the workshops weren't too busy at Stratford. The cabinet maker was available to make all the furniture. We could, perhaps, have used real things, but you'd have lost that uniform stamp. I was keen that the actual look of the pieces had a little of the feeling of the Swan itself. You were making things from scratch at the time when the Swan was being made – and it all felt as if it was being built just for you. It had a double non-reality: because you were in a theatre, and because the objects were being made as artefacts without a history. They were made for real, but because they were new you didn't have any sense of them as antiquarian pieces.

At first I couldn't understand a word of the play. John (Caird) gave it to me to read about three months before starting work on it. Thank goodness I had the nerve to say, 'I don't understand it, John'. In half-an-hour he'd taken me through the whole thing and I was hooting with laughter. It's remarkable that three months later, the same words spoken by actors, not only do not sound remote, they're actually very funny, witty and odd. It is most extraordinary. The brief from John was 'we must make this understandable now: we don't want a period play, or period costume'.

When you think of period plays, you think of people in funny costumes, and that was the one thing we had to leap over. It was a very special occasion, working in a unique theatre for the first time. We desperately wanted to make Elizabethan costumes understandable – clothes, rather than costumes. Luckily you have a long rehearsal period at the RSC, so I was actually able not to start the costumes until I'd seen the Company. And that was crucial. (See the costume designs on pages 57, 60, 92 and 93.)

I'm no Jonson expert, but is seems to me that there are two distinct sides to him. There's that whole low-life, everyday person. He's incredibly affectionate about that, and very comfortable. And then there's the poet. And that comes out in *The New Inn*. His observation of everyday life is unsurpassed – it's absolutely strong – and because that *was* so strong, you were able to deal with the poet without embarrassment. He had a great capacity for love and energy. He lived life in a real world, and then had the capacity to write the poetry as well. I suppose it's the same as Shakespeare, but with Shakespeare you don't tend to suppose that there was any other life. Whereas with Jonson, it's quite obvious he lived another life we'll probably never know about. I should give credit to John for the platform stage-within-a-stage in *The New Inn*. (See pages 94 and 97.) He knew he had to have a position on stage that was absolutely right for getting at all the house. And also, with so many people on stage, to be able to centre it. The Swan is a hard stage to block a piece on. Ideally it's a two-person stage – people will inevitably mask someone. You have to concentrate with Jonson, and constantly move people around, in order to keep the audience alert, and that is very difficult.

The Swan is built for Jonson more than Shakespeare. I don't imagine those plays working anywhere else. The intimacy of the Swan is like doing a radio play. And visually it all seems to be right as well. There's no reason to want to change it. *The New Inn* was a big set for that theatre. Geoff Locker had a real struggle to get the set on stage. Financially, it was a struggle. To have the capacity for seventeen actors to stand on one tread of a staircase cost money. It was a classic second-time-round set. I was thrilled with it, but in lots of ways I fell right into the trap that we probably knew was inevitable. In the first season we were happy to play on an empty stage, basically, but the following season we started to think that audiences had seen seven plays now, and we had better give them something to look at, something to put the light on. Yet some audiences thought that the set was actually part of the building, and I was very pleased about that. I knew I wanted more 'gut' than the actual Swan had. If we hadn't been in repertory, and could have done so, we would have broken into some of the actual galleries. They would have collapsed in, onto the stage. That idea might have taken over from the reality, finding technically what could be achieved, and what would marry into the Swan, with a few compromises on the way.

I found the Caroline setting and the platonic game-playing in *The New Inn* very heavy-handed on paper. But it is actually just a set-up to hear some of the speeches – and as long as you can relax with those then they're just wonderful. Both the comic and the serious, poetic sides of Jonson are very strong in this play. You could have set it in more of a fantasy land, but I think we'd have lost the sheer delight in Jonson by doing that. As with *Every Man In*, I had a chance to get to know the Company before designing the costumes. I wanted to keep the social distinctions between the characters, and to make them distinctive, without making them too fantasticated. I had total control over the fabrics to be used – their colour and weight – although sometimes budget has a lot to do with it, too. (Pages 18, 92 and 138.) Of course the costume for Pru was a deliberate allusion to Queen Elizabeth I. I'm sure that Jonson was merely avoiding prosecution by allowing Pru to represent the Queen. Actually, it's an interesting costume because it is really meant for the tailor's wife, Pinnacia, so one needs to design it for her, too. (See page 70.)

In *New Inn*, it was important to depict a whole cross-section of society. The height of the theatre helped, here, as well as the trap. People could be busy on several different levels at once. I suppose if one were doing a multi-million-dollar production one would have had a slice through a house – although it was possible to evoke that in the Swan, and to involve the audience-space, too. For example, the Host sitting in the pit to watch the game taking place.

It's important for the actors to feel close to the audience. The design for *Every Man In* had, at one stage, an idea of surrounding the edges of the stage with all sorts of objects, bonded together. What I hadn't realised was how much this would disturb the actors — this barrier between them and the audience. It wasn't very high, but it was enough to create a psychological barrier. The Company tried, very generously, to work with this at a preview. Then they asked if it could be taken away. I think they were probably right. The stage needs to be totally accessible. It's such a warm space.

The New Inn
Ben Jonson
Fiona Shaw as Lady Frampul and John Carlisle
as Lovel with the Guy Woolfenden song
(see p. 147).
PHOTOGRAPH: DONALD COOPER

JILL JOWETT

In my opinion, the best designs in the Swan have been those that have used little in the way of elaborate settings, stage cloths and hangings. The intimate space in that theatre, with its stage thrust into the audience, makes it possible to achieve striking visual effects in terms of colour and costumes (as in *The Two Noble Kinsmen* and *The Revenger's Tragedy*), with the minimum of scenic clutter. Some designers have successfully extended the natural ambience of the building (as in *The New Inn, Every Man in His Humour, Titus Andronicus* and *The Constant Couple*) and some have simply added a few versatile rostra (as for *The Rover* and *The Fair Maid of the West*).

Once a director and designer have agreed on the appropriate appearance for a production, the designer may choose to seek help from the Design Room. This is a service department for designers working in any of the three Stratford auditoria, and is run by a designer with fifteen years' experience at the RSC. It takes on a range of tasks, including model making, prop designing and drawing up, furniture and prop buying, and the sampling of substances and materials. It also undertakes set dressing, and taking technical notes to convey to the appropriate specialist departments.

The designers for the Swan have been a mixture of those new to the RSC and well-established designers who have worked in the Main House and The Other Place. The extent to which they have sought the help of the Design Room has depended to a large extent on their other design commitments. Bob Crowley, for instance, who helped to initiate the Design Room, uses its facilities and staff a great deal, and he is rarely working on fewer than two other major designs. New designers by contrast are often free to devote more of their own time to work on their productions, so that they need less auxiliary help.

Jill Jowett *first joined the RSC in 1962 but left to work with the designer, John Bury, and for the Belgrade Theatre, Coventry. She taught theatre design at Solihull Technical College before becoming Head of Art at the new Solihull Sixth-Form College. In 1977 she returned to the RSC and worked with John Napier, as well as doing freelance jobs. From 1981 she has been Design Assistant to the RSC in Stratford, setting up her own department to work alongside designers and production managers in all three auditoria.*

The Two Noble Kinsmen
Shakespeare and Fletcher
Theseus (*Peter Guinness*) marries Hippolyta (*Anna Nygh*) watched by Emilia (*Amanda Harris*) and attendants.
PHOTOGRAPH: JOE COCKS

Lord Beaufort

Lord Latimer

George Downright.

Jeremy Pearce.

The New Inn
Ben Jonson
Sue Blane's costume sketches for
Lord Beaufort (*Gregory Doran*) and
Lord Latimer (*Mike Dowling*).

Every Man In His Humour
Ben Jonson
Sue Blane's costume sketch for
George Downright (*Jeremy Pearce*).

Roger Formal

Mark Lindley

Justice Clement.

Raymond Bowers

Every Man In His Humour
Ben Jonson
Sue Blane's costume sketch for Roger Formal,
clerk to the Justice (*Mark Lindley*).

Every Man In His Humour
Ben Jonson
Sue Blane's costume sketch for Justice Clement
(*Raymond Bowers*).

9 *The Technical Scene*

GEOFF LOCKER

Geoff Locker *has been employed as Production Manager for the Swan Theatre since its opening in 1986. He had been with the RSC for ten years prior to taking up this position and has worked in the Royal Shakespeare Theatre and The Other Place in addition to having been responsible for managing productions of a number of tours both at home and abroad.*

The New Inn
Ben Jonson
Designed by Sue Blane. The Host (*Joseph O'Connor*) watches the action from the upper landing (centre), with Pierce (*Sean Pertwee*), Fly (*Clive Russell*) and Sir Glorius Tipto (*Richard McCabe*) left to right below.
PHOTOGRAPH: JOE COCKS

In the early days of planning the Swan, my own involvement was probably considerably clearer to the planners than it was to myself. A decision was taken that the Swan should be administered under the umbrella of the Royal Shakespeare Theatre, rather than employ its own administrator, as with The Pit and The Other Place. The employment of myself as Production Manager evolved through a process of dismissing a variety of other titles, in order to fit the job into an existing department, in this case the Production Office. Whatever else the job was to involve, Production Management would of necessity form the basis.

The number of staff employed to operate the Swan was carefully calculated to conform to the budgets available and to the scale of production to be mounted. Generally, these calculations have held good over the first three seasons. The theatre now directly employs two stage staff, two electricians, one Wardrobe Mistress, a Production Manager and two part-time Dressers. These staff are supplemented for performances and day-duties from other Royal Shakespeare Theatre departments as and when required, thereby not increasing the overall establishment. This system has the bonus of enabling Swan productions to avail themselves of the expertise available within the Company, particularly in the areas of Wigs and Make-up and Sound, without the need to employ such experienced personnel directly on a full-time basis.

Staff appointments were made only weeks before the first production was due on stage. It was a time when the auditorium resembled a building site, and most of us were still getting lost in the labyrinth of builders' corridors, wondering which way round the stage would go, and trying to make sense of the numerous permutations of what it might be made of, which were as diverse as hollow wood and solid concrete.

The constraints which had been applied to the staffing levels had then to be applied to the productions. Clearly there were financial limitations to observe, but perhaps the physical limitations of the building demanded the greatest inventiveness on both an artistic and a technical level. The 'get-in' for all scenery had to be via standard double fire doors. Storage of scenery and props was below stage via an opening not more than 8' 0" square, and at that time no scenery was to be stored in the auditorium. Coupled with this was the absolute necessity for changeovers to be achieved between matinee and evening performances, to keep abreast of the Main House repertoire, and accomplished by a staff of not more than six, including two casual helpers. These limitations have been imposed on every production since the theatre opened.

It is no accident that the Swan conspires to frustrate the efforts of anything but the simplest of stage settings. In his 'Plan for the Swan', Trevor Nunn spelled out his view of the way in which the theatre should operate. From a technical point of view, his plan still forms the basis of the only way in which the Theatre can continue without expanding its staffing, its budgets and its storage. Those early directives dictate that 'the key to the whole operation is that the internal design of the Theatre amounts to a permanent staging. Whilst design will have a vital significance in what we do there, it cannot be a design involving the changing of the configuration of the stage, or even of set building in the sense that we currently understand it. The Promontory stage and a back wall which continues the galleried features of the auditorium provide a sense of upper and inner Stage. It is the simplest possible structure on which to present the pre-proscenium plays of our dramatic tradition'.

The first and perhaps most influential appointment to the staff was that of Chief Electrician. The successful candidate was required to be an experienced lighting designer as well as a competent electrician, in order to offer his talents to incoming productions. The selection process was therefore a joint one between Technical Administration and Artistic Directorate. The position was advertised nationally, and drew a considerable response, but the successful candidate was found close to home in the form of Wayne Dowdeswell, who was at the time Chief Electrician at The Other Place. His initial task was to realise a suitable lighting rig from a modest budget allocation, and in a relatively short time, working under the guidance of the Royal Shakespeare Theatre Technical Systems Manager, who had been the Company's link with the architects in specifying the position of lighting bars, circuits and outlets. Between them, a very successful deal was set up with Strand Lighting to equip the Swan totally, and two hundred units were duly installed. The Galaxy lighting Board was chosen to allow compatability with other Royal Shakespeare Theatre systems, and an easier interchange of staffs, should the need arise. The system provides us with 276 working stage channels, plus 12 house-light channels to give maximum variety to the multi-purpose auditorium.

The principle on which the lighting rig was set up was that it should contain two-thirds fixed focus, and one third capable of being re-focused as necessary on the daily changeover. All incoming productions are dealt with on this basis, and additional 'specials' can normally only be achieved by acquiring extra equipment as a cost against each production budget. The budgeting system further discourages the employment of 'outside' lighting designers, in that they also become a charge to the production budget, thereby reducing monies available for other physical requirements. The Swan is fortunate in that the work of its resident Electrician has been well respected by production teams, and Wayne has taken responsibility for lighting all but three productions since the theatre opened.

It was never considered necessary to include any type of flying/lifting system in the architect's brief for the Swan, only the provision of a very few lifting points, primarily for light-

The stage set for *The New Inn*
Ben Jonson
Designer: Sue Blane.
PHOTOGRAPH: GEOFF LOCKER

ing bars. In the knowledge that any new production will invariably want the seemingly impossible, we should not perhaps have been surprised that Barry Kyle's opening production of *The Two Noble Kinsmen* required us to fly two actors in a metal cage eight feet above the stage, and once there, to play a particularly active scene. Although this went against what we understood to be the technical principles of the Swan, it was achieved with the use of an electric motor to considerable effect, and it remains one of the most memorable scenes of the past three seasons. (See pages 16 and 17.)

The requirement to lift actors or scenery provides one of the major headaches in trying to achieve designs in the Swan. Whilst trying to avoid the temptation to think of the theatre as too precious, there is an obvious reluctance to find too many fixings in the fabric of the building for the ever-increasing volume of scenery. Our efforts to postpone the day when the upstage wooden gallery totally disintegrates, through having held too many hinge plates, winches and brackets, has produced a continuing requirement for a versatile lifting system in the areas most used. This has never yet been achieved as a permanent part of the Swan, though the need continues to increase. We have managed since opening by installing equipment for each show as the requirement becomes known, but have continually frustrated our own efforts by the inclusion of equipment for play one in exactly the wrong place to manage an effect in play three.

Costume generally accounts for between 60% and 70% of a show's production budget. The actual amount depends on design and number of characters, but there is a pattern to expenditure-breakdown which rarely deviates from the norm. All costume work is undertaken in the Royal Shakespeare Theatre production wardrobe, under the supervision of Frances Roe, the Head of Department. There is an absolute standard to be maintained with Royal Shakespeare Theatre costumes and the intimacy of the Swan forbids any shortcuts. Actors often seen only from the front on larger proscenium stages are seen all around in the Swan, and attention to detail is therefore paramount.

Given the established commitment which Frances and her department must give to Main House productions, it is normally necessary to assess designs for Swan productions at least seven weeks in advance of the Dress Rehearsal. The first of these weeks will be spent sampling and buying materials with the designer, leaving six clear weeks in which to make and fit the costumes. Unfortunately, it is not always possible to have so much time. On occasion, a production may not be fully cast when it begins rehearsal, making necessary an initial degree of flexibility, often followed by a period of panic when the four week – no design stage is reached. When *Hyde Park* was mounted in the Swan to open the 1987 season, it was possible only to make the principal ladies' costumes. This situation arose partly due to a late design, through no fault of the designer, but more particularly through a huge volume of Main House work, which displaced the Swan production from the wardrobe workbenches. On this occasion, the entire set of costumes was hired from theatrical costumiers, and altered where necessary to fit. The result, considering the problem, was acceptable, but all of those involved felt that in other circumstances a better job could have been made of that production's costumes in our own workshops.

The scenery for all but two Swan productions has been made in the Royal Shakespeare Theatre Scenic Workshops under the guidance of Peter Pullinger, the Construction Manager. The continuity gained by a season's work being planned and realised through one workshop eases very considerably the otherwise difficult task of accommodating all demands, and ultimately allows greater freedom for designers to serve their respective productions. Anyone who saw the 1987 production of *The Jew of Malta* will no doubt recall the imaginative yet simple-looking setting designed by Bob Crowley. Its appearance was that of packing cases stacked floor to ceiling through the upstage galleries, yet as the play progressed they became a honeycomb of characters' houses, a bell tower, and a nunnery. (See page 84.) During the last scene, a huge drawbridge was achieved by lowering the vertical front section of the stack to the horizontal by use of a simple inbuilt counterweight system.

The realisation of this set and the ability to store and rebuild it throughout the season was perhaps one of the best examples of the collaboration between designer and technical/ construction staffs. In the confines of the Swan, this would have been considerably more difficult had the Royal Shakespeare Theatre Construction Department not been involved both in its making and in its adaptability to fit around the other shows in the repertoire. This example, however, is not to suggest that big use of working scenery is the only way to make an impact in the Swan. Sue Blane designed the most beautiful standing sets for the 1986 production of *Every Man in His Humour* and in 1987 for *The New Inn*. Her approach was much more sympathetic to the building generally. A great emphasis was placed on the smallest of details, whether scenic, costume or props. The intimacy of the Swan in my view responded extremely well to this approach.

Props used by actors in Swan productions tend to be very personal. They are items which, although eventually designed by the designer, tend to evolve through the rehearsal period, and be considerably influenced by the actor who will use them. This generally means that the Property Department are unable to begin making at the time they should, and makes it difficult to allocate a proportion of a Production Budget to a non-existent props list. For this reason, it is rarely possible to have a full set of props for the first stage rehearsal, and when they are ready they invariably have to be changed, however slightly, because someone forgot to pass on rehearsal information. William Lockwood, Head of the Property Department, has been responsible with his staff for producing some seven hundred props for the Swan over its first three seasons. Again, the collaboration between this department and the designer has achieved some remarkable pieces, ranging from a silver rose which drops its petals on cue, to an Elizabethan mousetrap which, though invented in house, could easily pass for a museum piece. Alongside these more intricate props is a mountain of furniture, most of which is specially made, a large number of set dressings, and numerous masks, normally cast from actors' faces. For *The Constant Couple*, designed by Ultz, which opened the 1988 season, the Department were responsible for making six scale models of buildings circa 1700, including St Paul's Cathedral, Buckingham House and the Royal Exchange. (See page 40.)

Staff in the Wigs and Make-up Department, under the guidance of Brenda Leedham, have produced wigs for most Swan productions, and notably the elaborate pieces worn in the

1987 production of *The Revenger's Tragedy* (see page 82), and those worn throughout the 1988 season of Restoration plays. They are created and maintained throughout the season to a very high standard. Others engaged in the daily routine which allows the Swan to function are the Stage and Props staffs, the staff of the Maintenance Wardrobe and of the Sound Department.

As a performance space the Swan has a considerable potential to turn itself around to provide a stage very different to the one we have seen in the first three years of operation. In 1988 we took the first tentative steps to foreshorten the stage for *The Plain Dealer*, by removing one metre from its length, and introducing a new mid level. This idea will be pursued for the 1988/89 Winter Season with an additional row of audience seating introduced in its place. We know that the stage height of 570mm is ideal to achieve the best sightlines for audiences in the stalls and the upper gallery, but efforts to keep coming up with something different will I suspect lead us one day to remove perhaps 4 metres from the length of the stage, to widen it over the upstage ends of the stalls, and to reinstate the displaced seats in front of the existing stalls seating.

In the 1987 Winter Season the Swan took in the Royal Court production of *The Road*. In order to accommodate this production, which was a promenade performance, it was necessary to remove all of the stalls-level seating and board over the whole auditorium. The result was interesting and successful, though I doubt if such a staging would be suitable for a Royal Shakespeare Theatre Swan season. It does, though, serve to highlight how adaptable this space can be.

The Swan, being new and wooden, has attracted its share of interest from the Licensing Authority and the Fire Authority, both during its construction and throughout its period of operation. It is a requirement that smoking is prohibited on stage, and to date we have been unable to use any form of naked flame during performance. Although now out of date, we still use the GLC regulations as our guideline, though generally speaking a degree of common sense applied to what one proposes to do on stage is all that is required. I await with interest, however, the day when Lady Macbeth has to descend the Swan stairs with an electric candle.

The Swan is now nearing the end of the 1988 season, and preparing to show its other face, playing host to a huge variety of visiting artists and touring companies in the six-week Winter Season. Its versatility makes it ideal as a performance space for a magician playing to children on a Thursday afternoon as much as for a full production of *Titus Andronicus* on a Friday or Saturday. It is a versatility to relish, and to extend, as the theatre makes its way into the future.

10 *Acting in the Swan*

TONY CHURCH

As an actor I had always been fascinated by the space that became the Swan auditorium, because I'd rehearsed in it for twenty years or so when it was the Conference Hall. Also, during 1965 I played a part in a massive exercise on the Greek theatre which was an internal activity we did at the end of a season and which involved quite a bit of performance in many audience relationships. It was clear that it was a remarkable space to perform in, even before the reconstruction. I was determined to get into the first production when it became the Swan. I got myself into the position of speaking, as Old Kno'well, what I thought were to be the first lines in the Swan (because there was talk of not doing the Prologue at that stage). Then they moved *Every Man In His Humour* to be the *second* play – and they put the Prologue in – so I lost that particular coup. But still I was there.

Joe Melia said a penetrating thing when he and I were watching what *was* the first play – *The Two Noble Kinsmen* – which I don't think actually cracked using the space properly. Joe said to me, 'I know what this place is, it's a Jacobean cabaret theatre. It's an intellectual cabaret theatre.' And certainly you chat to the audience like a cabaret comedian would use a cabaret audience. I was interested that he'd said cabaret, not music-hall or variety. Because that's chat, and it's quite intimate.

The Swan stage is extraordinary – I don't believe that there's another stage quite like it. The tongue of that thrust stage is narrow and long, whereas of course the Shakespearean stage was the other way round, approximately forty feet wide and thirty feet deep. Basically in *Every Man In His Humour* I *did* start the piece off in the sense of a solo person, walking onto the stage, going straight into an enormously long speech to the audience. That speech covered an enormous amount of ground, which set up the whole play. And then later in the play I had another long speech, which is a complete attempt to get the audience on complicit terms. In a proscenium theatre, when the whole audience is in front of you, it's impossible to involve them by talking to them. In a theatre where the audience goes round the sides, and you turn your head round, they know you're talking *to them*. It's as simple as that. Now the Swan has its own peculiar challenge which is quite formidable – and that is the height of the audience which is going round the sides. You have to make contact with the people at the extreme edges upstairs, and the nature of that contact is something that I found quite interesting to play with. The one thing that seemed to be perfectly clear was that in any piece of more than three or four lines at any sequence in the play, all the actors had at some point or another to get an eye up there. And when

Tony Church's *first professional performance was with a group of Cambridge actors directed by Peter Hall at the Arts Theatre, London. With Peter Hall and John Barton he founded the Elizabethan Theatre Company. He first joined the RSC in 1960, and played a number of roles with the company until he left in 1967 to become the first director of the Northcott Theatre, Exeter. He returned to the RSC in 1971 and has played numerous roles in Stratford and London, including the title role in* King Lear *(in the opening production at The Other Place, 1973). He is an associate actor of the RSC. In 1986 he played Old Kno'well in Ben Jonson's* Every Man In His Humour *at the Swan.*

you're playing a scene which has no direct address at all, you have to do some of the thinking with your head back and your eyes up into the corner – if you do, and you need only do it once in a sequence, then that audience is included.

It's part of the conspiracy of that building that the playing directions are strange. Because of the lay-out of the auditorium you can mask people very badly by standing right up at the corners. You can use the corners but they're not as dynamic as they are in other configurations. In the Swan you need to establish contact with the whole of the audience, and then to keep that contact dynamic. David Haig (Brainworm) had the longest direct audience contact in *Every Man In His Humour*, because he was always changing disguise and talking to the audience about it. Brainworm's role is really a sort of comic Richard III. Henry Goodman's role (as Kitely), which is obsessively jealous, depends for much of the comedy on talking to the audience. His was the real case of a part using the Swan as a cabaret theatre.

It was interesting that our sense of the cabaret-style actor-audience relationship had a direct effect on the design. In Sue Blane's original concept there was a melange of objects, all round the edge of the platform. When this element of the design found its way onto the stage in a preview the actors felt that it was a very bad thing. It cut us off. It created a mental, rather than a physical, barrier between us and the audience. So we asked Sue and John Caird to consider removing these objects. They did – and the difference to the performance was extraordinary.

Basically the Swan has an active·relationship with the audience. Whereas in the Cottesloe the space is verbally totally dead – like speaking in an old blanket – in the Swan the acoustic is live. You can't shout in the Swan – it bangs, and confuses the sound. But you can hit tremendously hard and it's dead accurate, like Brian Cox did with Titus. It's also good to be really quiet. The part of Titus has wild swings in it – from extreme comedy to extreme tragedy – and that building encompasses it. Providing the actor is accurate, and emotionally true, that theatre will take it. It's a very demanding house in terms of verbal control – it needs absolutely crisp and dead accurate articulation. The tuning is perfect for Jonson. Indeed, if you can speak Jonson's language I can't think of a better place to speak it in. Of course, Jonson *has* to have enormous energy. There is this bubbling, spewing geyser of energy which is partly intellectual and poetic, and partly really vulgar. Jonson is much more intellectual than Shakespeare. He's also much coarser – sometimes within the same line.

It's very interesting that Richard Eyre, for his production at The National Theatre, has translated the period of *Bartholomew Fair* into the Dickensian world. Dickens was, of course, Jonson's greatest admirer. He and his amateurs played *Every Man In His Humour* and Dickens himself was a famous Captain Bobadil. It was his favourite role – and what an extraordinary role it is – one of the greatest creations after Falstaff. The sheer over-do of Jonson is so amazing. I mean, to have a braggart, phoney soldier in a play, and then to have another man *play* a braggart, phoney soldier in the same piece. . . . There are so many things in that play that you think he can't possibly get away with. But he does! I think he got away with it because of the sheer richness of texture, and the sheer elemental energy of the whole creation of Brainworm. And Jonson's world is full of an extraordinary number of practical things. Jonson would put as many things as Shakespeare puts in a whole play in one scene – and more. The fight sequence seems to me the epitome of the problem of staging Jonson – it was essential to get it absolutely safe, and accurate, and yet it looked like chaos. It is like the sheer complexity of Jonson's script – it seems to have been conceived white hot. And once you get through the complexity to the tempo of real speech, real emotional pressure, then the mud seems to clarify. Similarly there were enormous numbers of detailed, solid props, built as real objects.

When we rehearsed *Every Man In His Humour*, John Caird encouraged each of us to do individual research into the society and ideas of Jonson's time. Thus he hoped to ensure the depth and texture of the production. It has got to go down to the root. Jonson himself was a man in touch with both the top and bottom of society. Jonson created real characters, not caricatures. They do have catch-phrases but they are very complex people. The humour was a *passion* – and if it was a passion then it could not be a mere caricature. *Every Man In His Humour* is a curious piece because it was virtually totally rewritten by Jonson himself. I don't think there has ever been a rewrite on anything like that scale. I mean to take, as Jonson did, the entire plot and all the characters and to rename the characters and rewrite virtually every single line – that must be the most unique work-over that anybody has ever done. To play Jonson needs a combination of open availability to the audience plus extreme character and situation accuracy. It does not allow for any smudge at all. So it is perfectly suited to the Swan. The Swan is a theatre that has got very clean lines. It's made of very clean fabrics – open, warm, natural wood, open brick, wooden floor. It's actually quite rigorous. You cannot put anything on stage that is untrue in any way.

It's the most demanding space I've worked in. But what it gives back to the actor, in terms of audience contact, is quite extraordinary. The best things that have been seen there used the theatre as it stands. In *Every Man In* my longest speech was out on the middle of Moorfields where there wasn't anything at all except a mile-post with a bird sitting on top of it. Although even there, there was constant traffic. The more one reads about what Moorfields was like, one finds that it was an extraordinarily busy place – I'm sure that's Jonson's type of place. It really existed – only a few minutes' walk from where the Barbican theatre is today. The play is saturated with a sense of a particular London environment. (See page 137.)

Jonson's plays have a sort of community life and morality. That came out clearly for the actors in the madrigal that we sang at the end, as part of the curtain call. It was the only music in the play. It became the emblem of the Company. We always met at the half-hour and sang the madrigal – it put us back in the frame. It came to be very special to us. And we restored the big speech of Young Kno'well on poetry, at the end of the play. Certainly it made a great difference for me, as Old Kno'well. Young Ed defends poetry in this bloody good speech – and Old Kno'well, a retired lawyer, reckons that he can't be all bad if he can defend his position in such a way. The speech is crucial – it comes from Jonson's heart.

Jeremy Irons *trained at the Bristol Old Vic Theatre School. His stage credits include Simon Gray's* The Rear Column *(director Harold Pinter), for which he won the Clarence Derwent Award,* Godspell *(playing opposite David Essex),* Tom Stoppard's The Real Thing, *winning the Drama League award and a Tony award, and, for the RSC,* Wild Oats *(playing Harry Thunder),* The Winter's Tale *(Leontes) and* Richard II *(Richard). He made his film debut in* Nijinsky, *and has since appeared in* The French Lieutenant's Woman *(Variety Club Award and British Academy Nomination),* Moonlighting, Betrayal *(screenplay by Harold Pinter) and recently* Dead Ringers *and* Chorus of Disapproval; *he has completed* Danny, The Champion of The World, *with his son in a leading rôle, and is making* Australia. *Television includes* The Pallisers *(BBC),* Love for Lydia *(LWT),* Langrishe Go Down *with Judi Dench (BBC), and* Brideshead Revisited *(Granada) for which he was nominated for an Emmy and won British Academy, Golden Globe and T.V. Academy awards. In the Swan he played Willmore in* The Rover *(1986).*

JEREMY IRONS

The Swan is a delightful space for the actor. You can communicate with the wink of an eye. Directors need to bear in mind that the space needs a lot of swirl, a lot of movement — which suited *The Rover* enormously. My feeling is that it is an ideal shape for a theatre — it is interesting that the Globe was not *that* different. As soon as you put Shakespeare on the Swan stage — I saw *Titus* there and I thought it was *so* immediate — it allows the actors, as it did with us in *The Rover*, to play far more subtly. In the Swan you don't need that 'Stratford style' of oration — of really banging it out. That style is not conducive to modern interpretations of Shakespeare.

There is a special atmosphere in the Swan. If you're not able to work *with* the audience it is a very difficult space. Henry Goodman, who played Kitely in *Every Man In His Humour*, used a very direct and easy connection with the audience. He didn't have to *do* a great deal — they knew exactly what he was up to. If an actor has a facility for that, the Swan is marvellous. The height of the auditorium must never be forgotten. It's really just a case of being athletic about it, and remembering that they're up there. In most theatres you are completely alone when you're on the stage — the audience is darkened — you are within your own life, within your own world. In the configuration of the Swan you are likely to be falling over handbags as you make your entrance. I suppose that is *their* world, and it can take you away from yours. If you relish that cross-over, as I do, it is very enjoyable. There *is* the actor — you can actually smell him as he goes past you. That immediacy is exciting — the very rub of theatre. I've always tried to keep an element of unpredictability in whatever show — whatever stage I'm on — in order to keep the show alive.

The Rover, with its carnival, its mask-wearing, its games playing, lent itself to such energy, and to the element of risk and surprise. (See page 27.) It's a very fragile little ship, *The Rover*. Indeed, one of the strengths of John Barton's direction lay in his ability to conceal the fragility of the play's plot and structure and to keep the action poised in a delicate balance. The production combined Aphra Behn's work with her source play, by Killigrew. John Barton had done the initial conflation — but as we worked on it during rehearsals we all agreed on various changes. Sometimes we found ourselves reverting to Behn's own work. It is a very complicated little machine, that play — even if it stutters in places. We went through a continual process of questioning and comparing. One of the principal achievements of the final version was the strengthening of the part of Angellica — and we were very lucky in having an actress of the stature of Sinead Cusack to play the role. (See page 153.) It allowed the play to *use* the contrasts between Angellica and Hellena. It was not even certain that Willmore *would* stay with Hellena, or she with him, until almost the last moments of the play.

IMOGEN STUBBS

The Swan is a brilliant space to work in. Although I haven't worked in very many, I've worked in either studio spaces or big theatres. For an actor, the Swan is the perfect intimate theatre. Almost all the audience are near you. They are within your eye-line, so that it deters them from fidgeting and fumbling, because they feel quite self-conscious, which is an advantage for an actor. But at the same time you're almost as prominent as in a film. On a big stage you know that if you fiddle with your hair or something, it's likely that most people won't see. That takes on enormous significance in the Swan. And that's very exciting. Whatever you do you're under scrutiny – and appreciated – even the smallest things you do.

I do find the Main Stage (I haven't done much there) quite difficult. You feel that because of the shape of it, it is in the worst sense like being on a big screen and whatever you do is part of an overall picture. It's either going to be embarrassingly big for the person you're playing opposite – which is a huge problem because you can't believe in each other's performances – or it's too big for the front rows and too small for the back rows. To find the right size on the big stage is very difficult. Also, because of television and film, and the fact that people are now so used to television, they start to get terribly restless in the big theatre, even if it's a good performance. People aren't trained as an audience to concentrate, and to suspend their disbelief. Whereas in the Swan they're thrown into it. I went to see *Titus Andronicus* and there were loads of really twitchy, bored children at the beginning, who became completely rivetted. It was like seeing people at a thriller, they got completely drawn in, whereas even if it had been as good on the main stage people would still have been eating crisps and getting the giggles and nudging each other, because they don't feel part of the experience of going to the play. At the Swan the audience has contributed half – more than half – the performance. And I think they know that. It makes people feel quite proud to have been there. If it's good they've made it good. Whereas at the Main House, whether it's good or bad the people feel very excluded and they don't feel that they make an evening – although they do. That's the worst thing. You *know* the audience feels irrelevant from how they're reacting, and in the Main House that's desperately important because you just lose heart.

At the Swan actors feel exposed if it's quite empty. But it's so wonderful if it's packed. And then it really does have that Elizabethan feel and it's like a really good party if it works well. In *The Rover*, when it worked well it felt wonderful. When it didn't work well, we felt very exposed, doing very silly things. When people went along with it, it was very rowdy, and a very funny evening.

So far as voice is concerned, you do have to be quite precise – otherwise it goes very fuzzy. But it's very much easier in terms of projection. You don't have to project it. If you *are* precise, you can whisper and people hear. It's a very testing place. In one way, it's

Imogen Stubbs *was educated at Oxford and the Royal Academy of Dramatic Art. Her theatre roles include* Cabaret *and* The Boyfriend *(Ipswich) and* Richard II *(RSC). She has made a number of television appearances including parts in* The Browning Version *and* The Rainbow *(Ursula), and her film credits include* Nanou, Summer Story *and* Eric, the Viking. *Her performances for the RSC in the Swan have been the Gaoler's Daughter in* The Two Noble Kinsmen *and Hellena in* The Rover, *both in the opening season.*

great to be thrown onto a bare stage and to have to act a real character. On the other side, apart from being very frightening, it would be very hard to keep doing plays with no set and a limited number of actors, and the same stage, exactly the same shape, and the same audience-actor relationship. You really have to fall back on your resources. If you did season after season like that, I think you'd long for some sort of gimmick to distract from what you're doing. I don't think the set should upstage the actors, which I think often happens on the Main House stage, but I think for actors you want some variation. I do think the Swan's the loveliest theatre I've ever worked in. But I don't know if I did eight plays in a row whether I'd be a bit tired of the same. . . .

The eye-line problem is difficult. You feel your head moving round all the time, like one of those dogs in the back of a car. You do it in order to take everyone into your vision, and that's really important. If you don't, people do feel excluded. Particularly people on the top. But if you do, people really appreciate it when you include them. In *The Two Noble Kinsmen* it was quite nice because I actually climbed up onto the eyeline of other people. That is hard. But on the big stage you have the phoniness of throwing everything outwards, even when you'd like to turn sideways. Whereas in the Swan every angle you aim in to another actor, you're taking in a whole new bit of the audience.

It's the business of exits and entrances that's hard at the Swan. You can't make flamboyant exits. They're clumsy. It's pretty clumsy getting onto the stage and off. It's a very limited perimeter. So you've got to make the audience believe there's an enormous amount of bustle. Deborah Warner does it very well through having a lot of activity, but you can't do every single play like that. And Trevor Nunn does it very well. But it would be interesting to see a play that demands a lot of pauses and a very languid pace to see whether people can cope with a lot of emptiness and silence. You do feel that you hold the audience in the hollow of your hand, and they hold you like that. If you can really get the concentration between you very good, then you can do anything. If they start looking at each other, that's agony.

When you exit you have to go through two doors and up some steps. And on the other side of the doors, you've got the other play happening in the Main House. There's an enormous bustle and mess behind there. You *hear* the Main House play – and its music. There were always people hoovering the bear [for *The Winter's Tale*] when we were doing *The Two Noble Kinsmen*. It's very hard to concentrate – there's nowhere to sit and concentrate on your character. Just a stream of people going to the café on the one side, and the dominating acting force of the Main House on the other side.

We did a lot of work in rehearsal on the connections between the Gaoler's Daughter and Emilia [in *Two Noble Kinsmen*]. The two basically have the same problem. They're two of the best girls' parts from that period. They came out more in London, somehow. The connection was emphasised right at the end where Emilia and the Gaoler's Daughter faced each other. We had something much more bold than that originally. We had something to do with pulling a hair through our teeth, and we shouted upwards, but we lost our nerve to do it. Barry [Kyle] had some really good ideas on a daring end. But the play didn't quite work itself up to a huge dramatic ending – so the audience couldn't take a huge final bang. The Gaoler's Daughter has a fascinating arc to the character – seven stages of one young girl's mental state. Infinitely more interesting than Ophelia. A terribly credible character for us, now, to believe in. The stages of her going mad, and the way people treat her, are beautifully written. Her lines are so simple, they're devastatingly touching: 'If you hurt me, I'll cry'. To be emotional and to speak Shakespeare is very difficult. But the Gaoler's Daughter is so simple. . . . (See page 112.)

Playing Hellena in *The Rover* was an altogether different experience. I don't think people would have enjoyed the original version before John Barton adapted it. The way we did it, it was a people's play. When we went to Newcastle it was extraordinarily popular with ordinary people – a 'Carry on up the Rover' production. It was fun to do. It's the difference between doing a play that's 'worthy' and accurate, and a play that people enjoy and you have fun doing. It got more camp as it went on. It's not real 'acting', but there was a good chemistry between the people on the stage. Jeremy Irons is a good person to act with. He has liquid eyes, and he reacts that moment off anything you do. And I act like that. I never do the same thing, quite. I like people to surprise me all the time. I like the challenge – which is very good for Hellena and Willmore. And Jeremy changes what he does the whole time, too. We were well suited. And it was a lovely cast. We changed the original script a lot, and most of it was made up between the lines. People playing the original script can't understand how we got it to work and to be so successful. Most of the energy and invention were put in by the company. It played almost as a Brian Rix farce. People objected because they thought it was meant to be very feminist – but it isn't. And it wouldn't have been.

At the Mermaid, you had to fight the theatre – the audience were antagonistic and disgruntled to start with. The Swan is friendly and warm. It's a lovely, cosy winter space. A Dickens adaptation would work well there. The Swan can cope with ambitious, unconventional projects. You need to surprise the audience – like *The Fair Maid of the West*, which is real popular theatre. It's hard to get Stratford people into the theatre. Maybe plays like the *The Rover* and *The Fair Maid of the West* will help do that.

The Rover
Aphra Behn
Callis (*Jenni George*), Valeria (*Hilary Townley*) and Hellena (*Imogen Stubbs*) in carnival costume.
PHOTOGRAPH: JOE COCKS

The Two Noble Kinsmen
Shakespeare and Fletcher
The Gaoler's Daughter (*Imogen Stubbs*).
PHOTOGRAPH: DONALD COOPER
(AT THE MERMAID THEATRE)

Titus Andronicus
William Shakespeare
Titus (*Brian Cox*) above, with Tamora (*Estelle Kohler*), as Revenge, and her sons Demetrius (*Piers Ibbotson*) and Chiron (*Richard McCabe*).
PHOTOGRAPH: JOE COCKS

Titus Andronicus
William Shakespeare
Set design Isabella Bywater. Lucius (*Derek Hutchinson*) with Aaron (*Peter Polycarpou*) captive.
PHOTOGRAPH: JOE COCKS

Titus Andronicus
William Shakespeare
Titus (*Brian Cox*) and his daughter, Lavinia
(*Sonia Ritter*).
PHOTOGRAPH: DONALD COOPER

Brian Cox *has played a variety of roles in seasons at the Edinburgh Lyceum, Birmingham, Nottingham, Manchester, Riverside and the National Theatre as well as at The Royal Court (where he won the 1984 SWET Best Actor in a New Play Award and 'Drama' Best Actor Award). He has appeared in a number of television programmes, films and radio broadcasts. His roles for the RSC have included* Danton in The Danton Affair, *John Tarleton in* Misalliance, *Timothy Bellboys in* A Penny for a Song, *Paul Cash in* Fashion *and Petruchio in* The Taming of the Shrew. *He played the title role in* Titus Andronicus *at the Swan (1987 season).*

BRIAN COX

When I agreed to do a season at Stratford for Terry Hands, it was very important to me that I had the opportunity to work in all three auditoria. The Swan is my personal favourite, simply because of the way it combines epic and intimate in very simple, clear ways. In the Swan you can be very simple in design and very direct in playing. It's very high and is sometimes difficult for an actor. But for certain moments in *Titus Andronicus* when the actor needs to soar – to be poetic, elaborate and rhetorical – that space worked very well. Equally it was possible to be very quiet. I think it's the best space at Stratford. The interesting thing is that it was based on the discoveries of the Company over many years, under the guidance of Trevor Nunn, that the real need was for a space that would accommodate a style of playing somewhere between that for The Other Place and that for the Main House. And I think the Swan has achieved that. Indeed, it's the best space of the new theatres. So many mistakes were made in the theatre buildings of the 1960s, many of which were designed by committees. We've either got tiny theatres (100–150 seats) or we've got epic spaces (seating over 1000). The Main Theatre at Stratford is virtually an Odeon theatre of the 1930s. But the middle ground is really what's needed in this country. The Swan fills that bill. And it fills the classical bill as well because in its thrust stage and its actor-audience relationship, it is essentially classic in structure. I think that the Swan is that very good middle ground, where you can still conceive a production in a very physical and a very stark way. It is like a miniature Shakespearean house.

Titus, I think, owed a lot of its success to the fact that we did it in the Swan – and it was the first Shakespeare in that auditorium. Deborah Warner is the natural director for the Swan because the work she does is essentially organic. (She is marvellous in The Other Place, too, as her *King John* demonstrates.)

Productions that are overburdened with design don't always work in The Swan. *Titus* had a very simple design by Isabella Bywater. She had an extraordinary grasp of that space, and of how to make the play work as part of it. The stage worked very much like an Elizabethan stage. We used the brick wall at the back of the stage and we used the bridge over the rear of the stage (see page 114). The design helped to give a real basis, rather than an overly-rhetorical basis, to the text. It helped to make the play available to an audience in the 1980s. I think productions of *Titus* in the past have failed from over-elaboration. They have tried to depict the decadent court in terms of the Roman films of Cecil B. de Mille. But in The Swan we could do it in a very stark way, in an auditorium that was physically sympathetic. It gave a quality of reality to all the suffering. There was a great discipline and visual simplicity in the design. Because there seemed to be no design, people thought that Isabella Bywater did nothing. But she worked closely with the Company and designed something quite brilliant. What she had was a sense of image. Like the simple image of Titus, sitting on the bridge at the back of the stage, under a bare electric light bulb, with Tamora as Revenge underneath the bridge, away from the audience. It's to do with disorientation and disconnection. An old man sitting, in a coat, on a stool, with a light: it's a very simple image. (See page 113.) The Swan lends itself to such simplicity wonderfully well. If I were a designer I'd be going more and more down the road of increasing simplicity.

The wood gives a sense of warmth to the Swan. The timber and other natural substances give it a very natural feeling. And it is sympathetic towards language-based plays – you suddenly *hear* Titus. When we worked on *Titus* we thought of it very simply – because we realised we had the Swan on our side. The audience was close. The Swan makes you available, as an actor, to the audience. You're immediately *there*, so you can be very sleight-of-hand. We were able to do things very simply, and have very simple visual ideas, like the entrance at the beginning with Titus carried on a ladder, and tables with white cloths – and then the image of Titus against the brick background. And humour, particularly the level of humour that we discovered in *Titus* – albeit black humour – is very accessible to the audience.

In *Titus* the first act consists of one long scene, and it is very much a scene in a public place. You can make the Swan audience the crowd, so when you walk in you literally play to the crowd. And that crowd doesn't go away – all of the play is conducted very publicly. Even when Titus turns on and kills his own son, that act too takes place in a public arena. You are still being watched, both from the bridge above the stage and from the auditorium. It's a wonderful combination of intimate and epic – because you're overhearing something that is going on in a public debating chamber. It would be a good space for *Julius Caesar*, in a way that the Main House can never be. Big theatres can make you lazy – in terms of presentation, and in terms of what you do as an audience. The Swan keeps you on your toes.

You can't get away with things. I remember seeing a production there, mid-way into its run, when the actors were getting a little cocky with it and were being a bit too intimate – it can't take that. There are disciplines which I believe are necessary. It is linked to my sense of what theatre should be – there's a kind of religious act going on – a ritualistic act. And such ritual needs structure and formality. The Swan has that. You have to be within your craft, and you have to be real – truthful. So that the skill of an actor is called upon. He can't be overly pyrotechnic, equally he can't be overly casual or domestic. The Swan requires a level of reality, and a level of concentration, which makes people focus onto that stage. It shares a lot with the other good theatre in this country, the Royal Exchange in Manchester. Both have that ability to reach people, no matter where they are, even if they are getting a bird's eye view. The Royal Exchange is though completely in-the-round, and I'm not altogether convinced that theatre-in-the-round works. I quite like the idea that you have *your* space, the space that you come from, which the audience is not privy to. Theatre needs to allow for sleight-of-hand. I like the magical effect of theatre, that is possible in the Swan – like the snapping of Lavinia's neck, or the cutting off of Titus' hand – but that also requires a special type of acting. The best actor I've ever seen in-the-round is Leo McKern. I saw him in a minor French comedy at the Royal Exchange and he acted so that whenever you were sitting at a point where he had his back to you the actual physical experience was completely real – you knew exactly what he was trying to convey, even from his back. Moments in *Titus* required that same physical concentration – particularly for the roles of Titus and Lavinia.

I think that the potential of the Swan is enormous. The lesson to be learned from it is that there is no reason why a theatre should not be designed properly, with a sympathetic auditorium. I've just been working in Moscow, where there are two Moscow Arts Theatres – one relatively new, a huge building, concrete and modern, with the seats all isolated from each other, and then the original Art-Deco theatre. Both seat over 1000 people. And yet the relationship between the members of the audience is much stronger in the original building, so that going to the theatre is much more a social event – a social happening. I think theatre needs to go back to that. And the Swan builds that rapport among the audience and between the audience and the actors, as well as focusing attention on that thrust stage. It's marvellous.

I hope that the Swan will be recognised for what it is. I think it will take a little time. The Swan has to grow as a house – and as an experience. It think it has had teething problems which are necessary teething problems. People have to get used to going to this middle house. I think it would be interesting to do some twentieth-century plays there, mixed with the popular Shakespeares – a *Hamlet* or an *Othello*. The plays I think should be done include some Ibsen and some Chekhov. It would be a wonderful house for those Ibsen plays that are epic in structure, like *Brand*, or *Peer Gynt*, or *When We Dead Awaken* – so that you could combine intimacy with stature. Also it would be very interesting to me to do plays like *Timon* – plays that need rehabilitation.

I think there are enormous potentials. Classic theatre spaces are classic for a reason – because people have found the best space for theatre. It is only when you allow economic and box-office concerns to dominate that you are in danger of ruining a good concept. The Swan is proof that you *can* have good theatre, and good theatre auditoria. The problem is getting people used to them.

Antony Sher *was born in South Africa, and came to England in 1968 to study at the Webber-Douglas Academy of Dramatic Art. He has played a range of roles in London (at the Royal Court, the National Theatre and in the West End as well as on television and film). He is an associate artist of the RSC and has played the Fool in* King Lear *and Shylock in* The Merchant of Venice *as well as leading roles in* Maydays, Red Noses, Tartuffe *and* Molière. *He took the title role in* Richard III, *about which he wrote* The Year of the King. *He played Vindice in Tourneur's* The Revenger's Tragedy *at the Swan in the 1987 season.*

ANTONY SHER

The Swan is a wonderful space to work in. I loved it. It's difficult at first. It's unusual and you have to get accustomed to it. I think it was about the third or fourth preview of *The Revenger's Tragedy* when Adrian Noble came to the show. We were still struggling to make it all work, and Adrian said something which I found very inspiring – and which proved to be absolutely true – that this theatre is like a camera, it can look right into your mind. It allows for very, very subtle acting. That peculiar wrap-around shape has the character of a kind of dissecting block, to be peered into very closely, and I think that is what's so special and wonderful about that space.

The height of the galleries at the Swan, right around the space, can present a problem – rather like that at The Royal Exchange in Manchester. I think that's a design problem which stems from the greed of fitting in too many seats. I wouldn't like to sit up there. It's difficult for an actor to play for the people in the top gallery because to reach them one would have to adopt stances which don't bear any relationship to human behaviour for the people sitting on the lower levels. Nevertheless, the Swan is easily the best auditorium at Stratford.

Vindice is a compelling character. He has been so very damaged by what has happened to him that the whole play is really a process of redemption for him. Although right at the end he is killed as well. It seems to me to be a very interesting piece of psychological writing, demonstrating how revenge is always a dangerous thing, something that people are pushed into doing. What's so very brilliant about the play is that Tourneur writes it as a comedy, and it's wildly, grotesquely funny in a way that's ahead of its time. It has one-liners in it that are like Joe Orton. The audience would constantly check with us afterwards whether we had slipped those in or whether they were in the script – lines like the Bastard's 'Old Dad, dead'. That gets a huge laugh and people just can't believe that Tourneur actually wrote that. Or the last few moments of the play when Lussurioso is dying, and as he's dying Vindice finally tells him the truth – saying 'Tell nobody'. It's terrifically funny in a grotesque way.

I very much liked Michael Levine's design for the production. He concentrated mainly on the costumes – on those wonderfully rancid, rotting costumes (see page 82). Because the play has to move around so much, in and out of the palace and all over the place, the Levine set was, I thought, built very cleverly. It was just a fairly abstract shape with a disintegrating curtain and a collapsed table sloping down (see page 81). The characters in that play are living in a very dangerous society and the whole shape of the set – the slanting table – was risky to run over. And there was a hole in the middle of the stage, with planks over it, that you felt people could fall into. That's why I think the design was so very clever – it captured the sense of danger and risk. And there was that wonderful tattered curtain that was like a literal representation of one of Vindice's speeches about night. That curtain evoked a cross between bridal drapes and a shroud. The lighting throughout the play also evoked a nocturnal world, that daylight never touched. At the heart of the tragedy is the sense that those people never go out. They're up debauching all night and never really see the daytime. I think the heavy candelabras, behind the curtains, were very evocative of that.

The success of the play depends on Vindice's disguise. At the beginning of the play I saw Vindice as a haggard, hermit-like figure, emerging from a hole, clutching the skull of his mistress. After all, for nine years he has kept that skull as his constant companion. Then he gets the chance to work his own revenge – and his disguise needs to be spectacularly good, so that his own mother and sister don't recognise him. That's important for the scenes in which he tempts them, too – they are difficult scenes, and as we worked on them it became apparent that there is an element of incest on Vindice's part towards his sister, and maybe even towards his mother, which makes the scenes absolutely gripping and quite unhealthy in a way. One gets the impression that this man has been so damaged by the tragedy of Gloriana that he is quite crazy, really. We worked very hard on his transformation. The disguise was to some extent influenced by the punk attitudes of today (see page 125). What finally released the part was the realisation that Vindice must have some kind of joy in it all, otherwise it's too ghastly to contemplate. It's a brilliant play because Tourneur has written it with great comedy. It's one of the problems – but when you solve it, that's what finally releases Vindice – finding that kind of joy.

John Carlisle *has played in numerous theatres and television shows. His roles for the RSC have included The King in* The Maid's Tragedy, *Apemantus in* Timon of Athens, *Parson in* The Fool, *Ulysses in* Troilus and Cressida, *Pastor/ Devil in* Peer Gynt, *Edward IV in* Richard III, *Canterbury/Burgundy in* Henry V, *Ralph Nickleby in* Nicholas Nickleby, *and Antonio in* The Merchant of Venice. *His roles in the Swan have been Machevil/Ferneze in* The Jew of Malta, *Lord Bonvile in* Hyde Park *and Lovel in* The New Inn.

JOHN CARLISLE

With *The New Inn*, a rare Jonson, you didn't have to build a set, the theatre *was* the set. We used all the galleries on all levels and we in fact used the auditorium in a small way as part of the acting area. So for me *The New Inn* worked very well in the Swan. But we haven't entirely discovered a way of playing the Swan in my view. The actors haven't. We're still playing something of a proscenium arch. We haven't found a way of playing to those galleries on either side; we're very aware that the bulk of the audience is in front; thrust out in front of us. And we tend to play to them in much the same way that we would in a proscenium arch. One thing for the future – the stage can either be lowered or raised, or used a little bit differently from the way it is at present. At the moment, nobody has done anything very much with it: that's the platform, and it's that platform that we use. And we tend to use it very austerely by having very little furniture. That's good. It's good not to be too fussy. But on the other hand there are areas where you can bring out the acting into different parts of the auditorium and make it a little more exciting.

John Caird was very brave in staging *The New Inn*. He designated as an acting area a small platform which was set quite a long way back from the middle of the stage. Our instincts as actors are always to play on the forestage. And that caused quite a lot of problems for some of the protagonists in that play. There were people who felt that they should not be playing so far back, and they felt it very strongly. And other people who felt that they wanted to be up there and displayed on that platform, and to use the whole thing.

When it came to *Hyde Park* you're taking a Caroline play and putting it, in our case, into a Bloomsbury setting. (See pages 28 and 128.) You've got to have furniture. You've got to have carpets. You've got the stage doing funny things: chandeliers coming out of the stage and being flown, and the stage opening to turn into a kind of little hillock or mound. That was much, much more of a problem to stage – and very few of us had any faith in it. It took a long time before we realised that we probably had the most successful play of the season, with *Hyde Park*.

The secret of The Other Place is that it has no personality. All it is, is a space where people sit. The building is saying absolutely nothing at all. In fact, you have to hide it a bit. All that there are, are rows of seats and an acting area. And so the focus is very very much on that acting area. You can feel that focus, when you come into the space. At the Swan, you're working in *a theatre*, and you are somewhat intimidated. It's not the Main House, where you've got to push right to the back wall. And it's not the intimate Other Place, where it's as if you've got little television cameras around you, and people can see the thoughts arriving in your eyes. The Swan falls between the two: and we're a little bit lost as to how far we can project, and how far we can bring the audience up close to us. I don't think we have found it yet – but it's a lovely exercise.

The Revenger's Tragedy (opposite)
Cyril Tourneur
Vindice (*Antony Sher*) in disguise as Piato.
PHOTOGRAPH: DONALD COOPER

The Jew of Malta (page 126)
Christopher Marlowe
Ferneze, Governor of Malta (*John Carlisle*) and Barabas (*Alun Armstrong*).
PHOTOGRAPH: DONALD COOPER

The Jew of Malta (page 127)
Christopher Marlowe
The Knights of Malta (*standing*) with their Governor, Ferneze (*John Carlisle*) on the right, and the Jews, led by Barabas (*Alun Armstrong, right*) seated.
PHOTOGRAPH: DONALD COOPER

Hyde Park
James Shirley
Mistress Bonavent (*Pippa Guard*) and Mistress
Carol (*Fiona Shaw*).
PHOTOGRAPH: JOE COCKS

Hyde Park
James Shirley
Lord Bonvile (*John Carlisle*) and Julietta (*Felicity Dean*).
PHOTOGRAPH: JOE COCKS

Theatres are like churches in a way. But I do think that an audience ought to have the feeling that anything could happen. There should be that excitement – that risk. There *is* an excitement in the Swan, a sense of being on the edge. . . .

There was certainly an element of personal risk for me as I was suspended high over the open stage-pit as Machevil. It was a most wonderful entrance. And I felt comfortable up there in relation to the audience, roughly on the level of the first gallery. That space had a tremendous feeling of command of the entire house. It was the natural focal point.

I found it helpful to double Machevil and Ferneze. After all here is this Jew, Barabas, a merchant who is doing rather well – and then he comes up against Christian morality. He comes up against Ferneze. And he hasn't got a hope. Because Ferneze is a Machiavel: the world *is* a Machiavellian world. And anybody who wants to live successfully in it must come to terms with Machevil. And so Barabas is driven to become a monster. Marlowe's imagery is very dangerous and very dark. Ferneze is the successful manipulator. I even tried to suggest that Ferneze was trying to do a deal with Del Bosco over Barabas's gold – although I'm not sure how well that was conveyed.

I'm hoping that directors and designers will become more adventurous with the Swan. Although it's hard to say what its future repertoire policy should be. The RSC have been playing big theatre for twenty odd years, very successfully, and we have a reputation for doing it well. We appeal to a very large slice of the middle classes, putting over Shakespeare pretty well. Indeed the initials RSC have come to stand for culture and civilised behaviour. When you put the RSC's name over The Other Place that same audience come to see what the RSC is doing in this little hut. And they get a shock: Edward Bond, Howard Barker, Howard Brenton. The RSC don't play to the converted in The Other Place, as the Royal Court or Soho Poly do. The RSC Main-House audience goes to The Other Place and gets a poet like Bond telling them where they are in society – it's quite shocking. I think it's healthy. I would hate to lose that. If The Other Place goes then perhaps the Swan should give that work a platform. Although I do agree that the Swan is ideally suited to sixteenth- and seventeenth-century plays.

Fiona Shaw *played a range of roles in theatre including Rosaline in* Love's Labour's Lost *(Bolton), Mary Shelley in* Bloody Poetry *(Leicester and Hampstead) and Julia in* The Rivals *(N.T.) before joining the RSC for whom she has played, among others, Beatrice in* Much Ado About Nothing, *Portia in* The Merchant of Venice *and Kate in* The Taming of the Shrew. *Her roles at the Swan have been Mistress Carol in* Hyde Park *and Lady Frampul in* The New Inn *both in the 1987 season.*

FIONA SHAW

The first thing about the Swan, apart from its obvious great beauty, is that it is a deceptive house. When you first sit in it – and when you first stand on the stage – you think it's going to be a great house, because of the relationship between audience and actor: it seems ideal. But the tiered system is quite a danger, and vocally you can think that you're controlling the house easily and you discover that you're not. I was very interested when I mentioned this to Cicely Berry (the RSC Voice Director) who said, 'Yes, it's a most deceptive house. It takes a lot more push than you think'.

Initially, when I worked there in *Hyde Park*, I felt how exposed we were. As the season went on, we discovered it was a wonderful house for comedy. I think part of that is that the audience's experience of going in there is so remarkable. You park your car somewhere by The Other Place and walk down to this beautiful building, by the river. I think this influences the very attitude of people when they sit in the Swan. I sat there myself to see *Titus*, and felt just gorgeous. Even before the show starts you feel wonderful in that lovely building. The wood is just so remarkable. The problem is that if you're doing warm plays and warm comedies, like *Hyde Park* or *The New Inn*, then the wood responds. I don't know whether that would always be ideal for other kinds of play.

Sue Blane's set was a triumph for *The New Inn* because she built the set like the Swan (see page 97). You couldn't transfer the set though, because nowhere else would have quite that impact. When we took it to Newcastle, it wasn't anywhere near as good. It didn't have that same completeness of a staircase built onto the stage and into the second floor, which the Swan had.

The Swan is the ideal-sized house. I'm not working there this year. But if I did go back, I'd go back for Shakespeare. That's all I wanted to do: Shakespeare at the Swan. We're in an age now who watch so much television and film that the size of an idea in Shakespeare is often too big for that tiny space. Here the Swan is ideal. You can deal with the idea without vocalizing the idea. You can explore the idea through a text on the stage. The voice and breath and size of image are ideal for the audience and for the person experiencing it. The problem about the Main House in Stratford is that it is glorious for certain great lines – the lines go across and arc and into that tunnel to the audience – you always have to look out to the audience, and that can be difficult. One has to set up a pattern where the other person always has to look at the person who is speaking, and then in turn when they speak the other person has to look at them, in order to appear as if you're having a conversation. But speaking across the stage is hopeless in the Main House, whereas in the Swan you don't have to worry about any of those things. You know Jonathan Miller's essay about boxing rings and theatres, and about theatrical illusion and cock-fight pits? The construction of a theatre, or an operating theatre, where you've got everybody focused into one area, has the effect of lending a kind of religious power at that centre.

And that's what the Swan has. It's not just because there are people in the pit that it's interesting at the Swan, it's because of the people round the edges looking down and in. They're putting energy back into the central hot-pot of the stage.

You are exposed when you perform on the Swan stage. But you're also focused. You're charged. You're exposed and you must use the energy. What happens in the Main House is that the energy is so easily dissipated. You can get away with murder; but it's much more difficult to be brilliant, too.

There are great problems of blocking in the Swan. You have to stay on the diagonal. And it's not just the diagonal. You have to do everything on the up-down line. The *Hyde Park* set was really too short. The best use of the Swan stage is when you use a space that goes behind the audience space, and when you use entrances through the audience. That's much better than cutting short on just that little postage stamp. Because you really need the diagonal. But even on the diagonal, in *Hyde Park* there was always someone in a seat who was being blocked.

Like a lot of bad plays, *Hyde Park* opened up the possibility for virtuosity. You have to have less respect for a bad play than you do for a good play. *Hyde Park* is not necessarily a *bad* play. But it is certainly a first-draft play. I feel ambivalent about the transfer to the Bloomsbury period. But on first reading the play it was so dense and so completely incomprehensible, that any aid to help it become accessible seemed a very good idea. I think the *next* production should be set in 1632. That should be fascinating.

Hyde Park has excellent parts for women. I suppose that's the other reason for doing it. The part of Mistress Carol is a link between Beatrice in *Much Ado* and Millament in *The Way of the World*. You've got a kind of arc of Restoration in England which, far from coming from France, had its seeds sown in England itself. The play is a fascinating little vignette from that point of view, and I loved doing it.

We rehearsed *Hyde Park* by doing a lot of little improvisations about the Bloomsbury period. We created various kinds of marriages. The point of setting it in that 1908 period was to be pre-war, and also that there was a period when people would themselves have been talking rather self-consciously. Because the play is quite self-consciously written. Already the language of 1908 seems to us a rather archaic way of speaking. Yet we began to speak the language so fluently by the time we got to London that I can hardly remember what it was like at the Swan. I remember it being at its best about June or July in the Swan. It was an extraordinary rehearsal period, because we created this whole world, on which we could sit the play. We could support it by this architectural dimension that would be recognisable.

The New Inn, by contrast, is the least successful play I've ever been involved with. I think it had a warmth due to that production, due to the set and the costumes (see page 138), but I never felt that we knew anything about the characters at all. It's an old man's play about a young man's world. I really dislike the play. I can see absolutely why it was a failure when it first came out. It is a very well-written bad play. It's bad because it's ultimately polemic. Its big speeches are ultimately manipulative. They're not really exploratory. They're not really complete. They're beautiful speeches – but bits of polemic. Jonson set up a construction where a man who is old and haggard and fed-up and cross and miserable, by speaking polemic about love, can get a young woman to fall in love with him. It's fantasy. Unexplored fantasy. The play should have explored the neurotic situation of Lady Frampul far more. You are talking about people who have got so far away from themselves that the metaphor really works, they really don't recognise each other. A man lives with his wife and doesn't recognise her.

I loathe Jonson's work and have no wish ever to do any of his plays again. Whatever his sensibility is, it doesn't reach me at all. No, I take that back – I think *Volpone* is a splendid, splendid play. Everyone was just mad about Jonson in Stratford, and thought he was the greatest thing. I just don't see *why* he is, that's all.

Hyde Park
James Shirley
Mistress Carol (*Fiona Shaw*).
PHOTOGRAPH: DONALD COOPER

Simon Russell Beale *has played roles for the Traverse Theatre and the Lyceum in Edinburgh as well as for the Royal Court. His work with the RSC has included the Young Shepherd in* The Winter's Tale, *Oliver in* The Art of Success, *Kuligin in* The Storm *and Nick in* Speculators. *He has played five roles in the Swan: Ed Kno'well in* Every Man in His Humour *and Fawcett in* The Fair Maid of the West *(both 1986 season); Clincher Senior in* The Constant Couple, *Sir Fopling Flutter in* The Man of Mode *and Lord Are in* Restoration *(all 1988 season).*

SIMON RUSSELL BEALE

The Swan is an individual theatre and one of the warmest theatres. In the first year it was terribly exciting. I have to say that the honeymoon period is probably over. I think that in fact it's quite a treacherous place to play. It's very exciting because of a very warm contact with the audience, absolutely direct. But technically it's very demanding. You need precision in volume. You can fool yourself into being more varied than in fact is feasible for that space. By the time I did my fifth production I was about as comfortable as I've been in any other theatre. It's a lovely feeling. This year is beginning to prove that there are problems in things like designing. I have a big worry that it's such a demanding place, it is such a unique theatre that the demands it makes might lead to every person ending up the same, every successful production ending up looking the same. We have a period now ahead of us where we are going to have to look very carefully at design. I'm sure you noticed from *Man of Mode* that the design hasn't been entirely successful and the set is unhelpful – because it dampens down the space. That particular space needs to be shone up. If you overdesign, you end up by destroying the particular quality of the theatre.

The same thing applies to actors of course. The type of precision work that you have to do, you end up doing the same thing again and again. The same type of high, light, sharp kind of speaking. Oh God for a bit of whispering or bellowing. The Other Place is always a luxury to work in because it's so intimate, and actors always love that, the feeling they're really acting, internalising. The Swan Theatre is a display theatre in a way that even the Main House isn't. The best bits of the Restoration plays this season are the bits where the displays are fully accepted by the actors and they've gone full out for it. You can't really do that sort of display at The Other Place. The transfer of *Every Man In* to the Mermaid didn't work because we were relying on the personality of the theatre. *Every Man In* was frankly appalling at the Mermaid because the Swan had provided 50% of the warmth of that production. Some of the performances fell victim to the sheer hard work of trying to get to the back of that very very deep Mermaid auditorium. The wonderful thing about the Swan is that it has no depth at all.

I've done more Jonson than Shakespeare. I'm a great fan of his. He's absolutely marvellous to act and the reason why it worked so well in the Swan is because he has a quality of upgraded naturalism, a sort of heightened naturalism. The Swan is absolutely ideal for this because you can use the intimacy at the same time as doing the display. If you play a part like Bobadil, that enormous display part, at the same time you have to be able to drop it down to utter naturalism. Jonson demands it and that's why he's so suited to that theatre. I remember thinking that we should call it the Jonson theatre. It would be wonderful to see a *Volpone* there, and it would be wonderful to see an *Epicoene* there. Perhaps *Volpone* might be a bit strong, a bit heavy, a bit poetic.

You can't hide on the Swan stage. I know that sounds pretentious but you can't. There are theatres you can. You can hide on the Main Stage very easily indeed. You can't in the Swan. I had a big aria in *Every Man In*, that big speech at the end, the poetry speech, very heartfelt and moving, and you thought you saw Jonson sitting there on your shoulder. It was always difficult for me because I couldn't hide behind the character. I had to expose *me*.

The Constant Couple is a 'cool' play. I am at odds with almost every single critic about this. We've been accused of sacrificing social commentary for a type of cool and elegant performance. I think we're right. Roger (Michell) and I decided at the beginning to do the Newgate scene quite seriously because we felt at least here's one scene of emotional engagement. As the run has progressed – I don't know whether it's because of the way we've done the rest of the play, I don't think it is – it has had to be played cooler and funnier, to give the audience a chance *not* to relate to the emotional state of the character. In fact the earlier interpretation was forcing the scene into a mould where it wouldn't go. I think that applies also to the Lady Lurewell scene with Jenni (George) when she describes being raped, being seduced at sixteen. I don't think the play deals very seriously with those situations. There's no point in pretending that Farquhar in that very early play was doing something that required extraordinarily detailed personal observation. *Man of Mode* is a different question, but *Constant Couple* is I think very cool and clipped and young.

The set design supported this interpretation. In that particular warm space, David (the designer, Ultz) wanted to change the colour of the wood – which he did. He lightened the floor so that instead of being golden, it was a lemony colour. The models of London buildings were all very light wood. (See page 40.) He's done the play a great service. The wonderful and inspiring thing about the Restoration season, despite all the gruesome mistakes, on the positive side we have come up with some extraordinarily brave and detailed commentaries on the Restoration, on a genre that has been neglected. The role of the Fop may seem a very conventional and predictable one. But when you sit down and read the parts you find things out, for example that Clincher has a moment in the play when without any posing he discusses his problems and his feelings. That's unheard of. Fopling is actually stupid simultaneously and sad. He has an emotional life – where he sings, for example. This was one of those scenes which because of the work we'd done didn't have to be rehearsed at all. Gary (Hynes) said, 'It's six o'clock in the morning, you're hung-over or drunk, you come into someone's house and he's just had sex with a woman.' Immediately, with all the work you've done about Sir Fopling being lonely and a loner, you suddenly become lonely in that scene. It was an amazing intellectual journey.

The wonderful thing about the songs in *Man of Mode* is the general rule about the Swan really, that recorded music does not work, and you have to have a live band. I think it's become a hallmark of the Swan. We had one recorded sound cue in *Man of Mode* – that was the only sound cue and it felt quite peculiar.

Every Man In His Humour
Ben Jonson
Ed Kno'well (*Simon Russell Beale*) behind the
disguised Brainworm (*David Haig*), with Master
Stephen (*Paul Greenwood*) at the crossroads.
PHOTOGRAPH: JOE COCKS

Lady Frampul

The New Inn
Ben Jonson
Sue Blane's costume sketch for Lady Frampul
(*Fiona Shaw*).

The Man of Mode
George Etherege
Simon Russell Beale as Sir Fopling Flutter
(*centre*).
PHOTOGRAPH: JOE COCKS

Joe Melia's roles with the RSC include Ubell Untermeyer in Section 9, Froylan in The Bewitched, Bill in The Can-Opener, Sgt. Fielding in Too True to be Good, John Dory in Wild Oats, Len Bonny in Privates on Parade, Touchstone in As You Like It, Thersites in Troilus and Cressida, Autolycus in The Winter's Tale, Robert Walpole in The Art of Success and the Chief of Police in The Balcony. At the Swan he played the Mayor and the King of Fez in The Fair Maid of the West (1986 season) and returned in 1988 to play Alderman Smuggler in The Constant Couple, Old Bellair in The Man of Mode and Parson in Restoration.

JOE MELIA

The Swan is the first thrust stage I've ever been on, which is so much more thrust than width. Which means that you've got this wonderful immediate relationship with the audience, like an Elizabethan Talk-of-the-Town, a cabaret-cum-supper-cum-theatre. But from an actor-orientation point of view, the actor finds himself wanting, in spite of himself, to play to where the natural proscenium-arch focus is. In the Swan you are consistently wanting to play towards the apse. But if you think about it, because the thrust stage goes so far forward, there are as many people at the sides (and stacked up) as there are out front. In a play like *Fair Maid* it didn't matter, because Trevor (Nunn) used every inch of that stage, and we actually rehearsed on the stage from day one. He was always saying 'give *them* a bit'. The production had a kind of machine-gun technique – there was so much going on – that if an audience missed one gag there was another, if they missed one bit of information it would be repeated. And that's fine. So you get a wonderful whirligig. And I took it for granted that that's the way the theatre was. But then I thought, you can't do them all like *Fair Maid* – a sort of Elizabethan pot-boiler or pantomime. What happens with texts with specific moments? They could create difficulties. In *The Constant Couple*, all the scenes are two-and-three-handers except for the big dénouement scene. If you come too far forward you give people on the sides a constant back view and you can block other actors from the front. So you have to keep it fluid. And that can detract from the effect if you need a still moment. It's like theatre-in-the-round, which never seems to me to work. All theatres have drawbacks.

The other problem is that in Elizabethan plays there is a kind of Brechtian style. You come on quickly (a drum, a banner and you're there) and then the words paint the scene. Some of the Restoration plays really do postulate *interiors*, real detailed interiors. In the opening scene in *The Man of Mode*, there is a kind of limbo – because you can't put trucks on. There is a real *setting* problem. There are scenes with a swirling drawing room, and then sudden close-ups of two people having a very private conversation – in what is, after all, a very public theatre. Probably the answer is for the two people who are talking *not* to be private, but for the rest of the people on stage not to notice them (so indicating their privacy). It has to be kept up and out.

On the Restoration stage the two 'private' characters would be on the apron, speaking to the audience from the front. You can't do that in the Swan. There is another problem of 'realism'. Sometimes you have to seem to be carrying on a conversation for which there are no lines, and yet you are very close to some of the audience – almost too close to convince them. You need to keep something going. You can't get lost. In *The Man of Mode* there's a tendency to stand back against the back screens simply to avoid blocking people. Also, in the front corners, there's a tendency to turn towards the apse all the time – but if you look upstage you can actually take in a largish section of the audience. You mustn't exclude the *same* people all the time. In *The Fair Maid*, the constant movement, and the Elizabethan-tavern-like ambience, countered this.

I don't want to knock the Swan, but after the first careless rapture it's helpful to look at the problems. You've got to look at the problem of design in that theatre. At the beginning I thought there would be no design, perhaps rather Joan Littlewood-ish. I imagined ten actors coming on with a skip, banging it down and tossing out the costumes. But you can't keep repeating that. Yet once you start building proscenium-arch backdrops you compound the problems. The building is a cosy sketch. When you bring on a banner, the banner really counts. When you bring on a uniform it's bound to be significant. It's very Brechtian in that sense.

The Jonson plays actually used the building, and it blended. John Napier used so little (in *The Fair Maid of The West*) – the curtain became the sail – and people loved it. (See pages 58 and 59.) They need to do their part. *The Fair Maid* worked in the other buildings, too – although it's more difficult to 'take over' the Mermaid in quite the same way, even though we actually took the stage with us!

The Fair Maid of The West
Thomas Heywood
Imelda Staunton as Bess Bridges and *Joe Melia* as King Mullisheg, of Fez.
PHOTOGRAPH: MICHAEL LE POER TRENCH

11 *The Music of the Swan*

GUY WOOLFENDEN

Guy Woolfenden *is Head of Music for the RSC. He has composed over 120 scores for the Company, as well as scores for productions at the Comédie Française, the Burgtheater, the Teatro di Stabile and Den Nationale Scene, Bergen. He has also composed for television and ballet, and conducted for the Scottish National Opera as well as with major symphony orchestras in the UK and abroad.*

I've known the space, when it was called the Conference Hall, for over twenty-five years, and we suspected all along that it would have a wonderful acoustic, if it were rebuilt in some other form than a rehearsal room. In fact, it used to be said that there were plans to use the space as a sort of stand-by broadcasting studio in case London got bombed during the war. I don't know how much truth there is in that, but the walls were clad with sound-absorbent 'peg-boarding'. (See page 8.) We suspected that the acoustic had the potential to be rather remarkable when the new building was completed and, for my money, so it has proved. The natural acoustic in the Swan is wonderful – and I've experienced everything from the speaking voice to the London Mozart Players, including song, madrigals, a string quartet and a brass quintet, and it has never let us down once. The only problem is when a director or designer decides to build large sets in front of the musicians, and then asks for amplification. I personally think that is daft.

For the first production, *The Two Noble Kinsmen*, we placed musicians where it seemed natural for them to be, that is, in the second gallery, dead centre, right across and above the back of the stage. For *The New Inn*, the musicians were also a visible and integrated part of the production. While it is possible to involve musicians playing from memory, in costume, on stage in the Main House, this technique has lapsed over the years, so to have a building like the Swan which has a natural acoustic that you couldn't really improve on, and then to deny musicians contact with the audience visually, as well as aurally, is crazy. One production I would exonerate from that rebuke is *The Revenger's Tragedy*, because Di Trevis wanted a strange distorted sound, so the music, which was scored for two bassoons, bass clarinet and percussion, was fed through the speaker system and electronically treated.

The Swan does not have a fixed ensemble of musicians: for example, a violin, 'cello and harpsichord. We have no set policy about what sounds each production should have. This is totally in the RSC tradition, and personally I fully support it. There *is*, however, a policy for funding the musicians. We are guaranteed for every production in the Swan (if the director and composer want it)'three musicians. And then the horse-trading begins. Every Swan show plays against a Main House production and possibly one at The Other Place. When the needs for those two other theatres have been sorted out and haggled over, lobbying begins from the chosen composer of the Swan show. For example, in *Hyde Park* the composer Jeremy Sands desperately wanted a flute and a clarinet in addition to the three he was allowed, so that his line-up was flute, clarinet, trumpet (doubling cornet),

Guy Woolfenden's setting for the Epithalamium that opens *The Two Noble Kinsmen,* sung (at alternate performances) by boy sopranos James Lowry and Robert Willey.

'cello and percussion. I was writing the Main House show, *Julius Caesar*, that played against *Hyde Park* and with a little bit of arm-twisting, I dropped my flute and clarinet. It is usually possible to work something out. Just occasionally you come across a director, like Deborah Warner, who has just won the Olivier Award for *Titus Andronicus*, who could have had four or five musicians if she had wished. When we started talking seriously about the music, she was extremely reserved and sceptical, saying, 'I don't know, it's not the way I work'. I tried to explain the policy and even offered an experimental rehearsal. But, bless her, she stuck to her guns and did the whole show without any professional music (although she did use two actors banging timpani at moments of tension). At one point she said, 'I would be embarrassed to have professional musicians in this show, because there would be so little for them to do'. There was no union problem, because for musicians it simply meant a night off instead of losing any work. After that I worked with her on *King John* (The Other Place) and we got on very well together – so well, that when the same production of *Titus* transferred to The Pit (at the Barbican), she asked me to write music for it. I am convinced that the music has added another dimension to an already magnificent production.

We have also used the singing voice in the Swan, for example in the two Ben Jonson plays and, of course, the very first music in the Swan was the boy's solo voice for the epithalamium at the beginning of *The Two Noble Kinsmen* (see pages 144 and 145). He was standing in the second gallery, stage right, to sing this wedding hymn (that almost turns to a requiem when the widowed queens come in). The scoring included two horns (often mentioned in the script), flute, bassoon, percussion and a harp. The clue for the inclusion of a harp came from the reference in the script to 'a sudden twang of instruments' when the hart appears as Emilia prays to Diana. I was slightly disappointed that Barry Kyle didn't have the little boy leading the procession and strewing petals as suggested in the stage directions, but I appreciated the difficulties. I have since discovered that other composers have used the same lyric ('Roses, their sharp spines being gone') for moments when Shakespeare lets you down, that is to say, when he indicates a song without writing a lyric! I deliberately didn't incorporate too much oriental flavour into the music, in spite of the clues in Bob Crowley's designs. We did, however, experiment a great deal during rehearsal with the music. For example, Barry Kyle found a recorded oriental dirge and we worked on that and adapted a version of it for the production.

So far, directors in the Swan, even though we have the facilities, have not used recorded sound effects to any great extent. There is something about the building that makes them appear phoney, unless they are brilliantly and carefully used. The only exception was *Every Man In His Humour* where the director John Caird did use the sounds of London life, which were skilfully integrated into the production. He also decided not to have any instrumental music, but thought, as a sort of present to the audience at the end of a rich and rewarding evening, it would be a rather charming idea if we offered a madrigal called 'In Going to my Naked Bed', the sub-text of which, if not the actual lyrics, is curiously relevant to the play. I rehearsed it with the cast and Simon Russell Beale, who is a fine musician as well as a gifted actor, conducted the cast at the conclusion of the curtain calls.

Guy Woolfenden's original music for the song
at the end of *The New Inn*.

In *The New Inn* there is a key moment for a song, in that the lyric for 'it was a beauty that I saw' is written before our eyes, polished, and then presented at the end of the play (see page 147). So you can't duck it. It would be unthinkable to have a production of *The New Inn* without music. The most important person, that is the author, Ben Jonson, asks for music at many moments. He refers specifically to 'fiddles'. We also started magically and mystically with another song from Jonson in the play: 'Is this a Dream?' It was a welcoming song – welcoming you, the audience, to this strange inn, where many things would be revealed. I used a rough pub ensemble with the two fiddles mentioned by Johnson, a percussion player and a bass line from the bassoon. They were free to roam and ramble all over the set if they wanted, but they also had a fixed position, from where they were visible, but not distracting, to the audience. If you can see a musician play, you actually concentrate on the music more intently.

I did a great deal of research into the music that Ben Jonson would have known. He wrote more masques than anybody and I researched into those using Mary Chan's book on the music for his masques. In *The New Inn* there is one long sequence of music that had to be very quiet (off-stage or quiet music in the Swan is very difficult). We finally went into the 'amplifier room' on the second level and we even used the door as a swell pedal. The whole of that sequence was adapted from the music from one of Jonson's masques. We were, after all, involved in only the fourth professional performance of the play in history, so I felt we should at least look at the music that Ben would have recognised and approved of.

In *The Rover*, the music was very much complementary to the carnival atmosphere which was inherent in John Barton's direction of the play. The problem was that the play was set in some sort of vague Spanish colony, even more vague than in Aphra Behn's play, since John incorporated some of the Killigrew source play. We wanted something exotic. We also wanted something that could support the military side of the characters like Willmore and Belville. We also wanted something that could sound *mardi gras*. The problem was that there were just three musicians! And so I chose a trumpet, an electronic keyboard (which can be very versatile) and percussion. John is always keen to establish five or six key tunes which he uses as leitmotifs and encourages his composers to develop the incidental music from the songs if there are any. *The Rover* text contains several little drinking songs which the soldiers sing and, once John and I were happy about the melodies for those, the whole score could expand out from them. There were also various festive dance tunes.

The largest group of musicians we've ever used in the Swan was for *The Fair Maid of the West*, which had a great number of songs and dances and a composer completely new to us, Shaun Davey. Trevor Nunn had an idea that there should be some Irish influence in the music. Originally he wanted The Chieftains to write and perform the music, but it was impossible for them to fit into the repertory situation! They recommended the composer, and we were able to field a band of nine musicians: flute, oboe (doubling harmonium), bassoon, violin, 'cello, guitar, harp, Uileann pipes (doubling trumpet) and percussion. That was a tremendous thrill, and Shaun Davey's excellent score, enhanced by Imelda Staunton's singing, sounded superb in the Swan's fine acoustic.

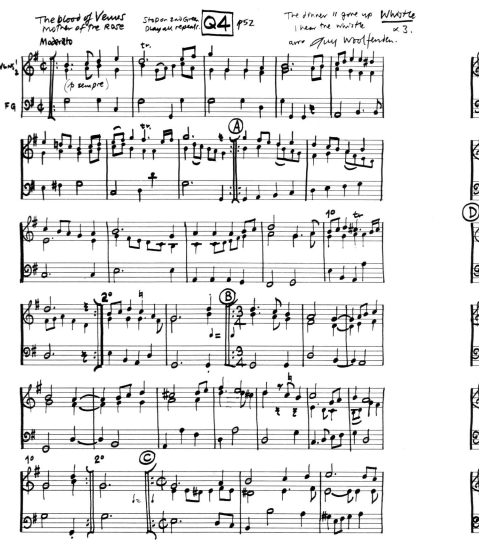

Guy Woolfenden's music for Act Three,
Scene One, of Ben Jonson's *The New Inn*, at the
cue: *Jordan*. The dinner is gone up. *Jug*. I hear
the whistle. *Jordan*. Aye, and the fiddlers.

The Rover
Aphra Behn
Frederick (*Peter Guinness*) and Willmore (*Jeremy Irons*) with carnival masks.
PHOTOGRAPH: DONALD COOPER

12 *Voice and the Swan*

CICELY BERRY

Cicely Berry *is Voice Director of the RSC. She has many years' experience training actors and teachers at the Central School of Speech and Drama and running her own studio in the West End. With the RSC she works with actors involved in all the Company's productions both in Stratford and London. She also takes an active part in the RSC's links with education. She has written about her methods in* Voice and the Actor *(1973) and in* The Actor and His Text *(1987).*

When we first worked in the Swan, for Barry Kyle's production of *The Two Noble Kinsmen*, the space was an unknown quantity and we were quite anxious about it. Actually the acoustics are very good, but as in any space, there are certain problems – you have to know how to use it, where the good places for speaking are, and where it gets a bit dicey.

In this space, the problem is to do with the audience being all round, so that immediately you turn your back on one part of the audience and face one side, the people behind you will find it difficult to hear. Also it is very high, and the danger areas are particularly for those sitting at the top and sides: they are looking right down at the actors and cannot see their faces, and when you can't see someone fully you feel that you can't hear them. It's a psychological factor that if you don't see you think you can't hear. That area is a very difficult one. So we get some people very near, and some people a long way away, and also the problems of the thrust stage, so that if you are forward or facing one way, you will always have your back to someone. So what do we do about it? You can't just speak loud or the people in front of you will get blasted, and anyway the character will lose credibility, it will not seem natural. The answer is in the energy of the consonants: you have to be very clearly spoken, not loud, but really clear. And by this I don't mean over-emphasising the consonants, I mean feeling their energy and through that the energy of the language – and finishing them off properly. You have to really think about the words and feel that energy carrying forward, consciously.

I think the space does not take a low voice well, low in pitch I mean; but then The Other Place doesn't either. The voice has to be lifted outwards. If you drop the ends of lines they get lost.

Andrew Wade and I have worked on all the plays in the Swan, but to different extents. The Main House plays always take priority, and often need most of the time available. There has been a very wide range of plays in the Swan, plays which need a great deal of preparatory language work, i.e. not just work on clarity but on how the language works – their rhythms and syntax. The Restoration plays we have done this year I think needed that preparatory work particularly, and certainly they needed more work than we were able to do in the time. I don't think we really cracked the speaking of them at the outset, though I think now, having played them for a season, they are very good. The language takes time to live with. In these plays the style is more self-conscious: the actor needs to feel through the language but to present it at the same time, and this is difficult. This sense of 'presenting' language, yet keeping it real is crucial. Restoration plays have far more emotional reality in the characters than is often believed, yet the refinement and veneer are crucial and have to be consciously played. It is a very fine balance that has to be found. What is difficult is that the argument works cumulatively, and is in itself an expression of an emotional reality. Nowadays we have a tendency to separate our emotion and our argument, but in Restoration writing these are inseparable, and this is what makes it a problem for a modern actor. I think we now have preconceptions of how the language should be spoken, with all the flourishes and conceits, and it is difficult to get back to the character's necessity to express himself in that way. I worked very closely with Garry Hynes on *The Man of Mode*, who was very eager to stress this emotional reality – that the extravagance of the language was not to do with superficiality, but with a genuine need to express in that mode. The style was the reality, the content.

In some ways Ben Jonson anticipated some aspects of Restoration language. When you first read it, it is difficult to make sense of it, but when you start working on it the verbal energy releases the meaning. Tourneur's language has an emotional richness. This may sound ridiculous, but in a sense Shakespeare's language is easier to deal with. There is an underlying emotional continuity and rhythm which makes it easy to speak, and sometimes this is a trap. I suppose anyway Shakespeare's language and habits of mind are somehow more familiar – they seem more modern. I work a lot with young people, and I am fascinated by the fact that very often the low-ability, and less highly-educated children get more quickly to the emotional root of the language than those who are more sophisticated. It is something to do with the availability of the images and the rhythm.

Basically, I work on all the plays in the same way, whether they are Shakespeare, Jacobean or Restoration. My work is based on finding the rhythm of the language, and how that rhythm releases the sense. I do a lot of work moving with the phrases and thought. The more you find the movement and the different rhythm-patterns, the quicker you find the emotional force of the writing and the linking of ideas. It is the key to how speeches work. It is important to find out how one thought leads to another, and how the thoughts are of different lengths. Many actors, for instance, find Jonson's language difficult to unravel, but when you work on it with movement it becomes clear. So for example the long arias in *Every Man In His Humour* become quite natural as they emerge out of the texture of the play. I do believe that one misses about 60% of the meaning of a play if you do not work on it out loud.

There is of course a very different texture to the language of Shakespeare and of Jonson: this is easy to sense. Jonson's language is much more splintered, and the changes more sudden and vigorous. It has to do with the vision of the writer, because how each person expresses himself is totally to do with that person's thought-process. Something underlies the work of each playwright. The sound is distinctive to each writer. However skilful he is in creating individual and even idiosyncratic characters, there is a sound which we recognise. And that distinctive quality of the playwright is traceable in the speech

The Rover
Aphra Behn
Willmore (*Jeremy Irons*) and the courtesan
Angellica Bianca (*Sinead Cusack*).
PHOTOGRAPH: JOE COCKS

patterns. The actor has to be very open to this, very aware, to listen for the different music. Jonson is a more subjective writer, more personal. His humours are passions and he feels them deeply. You have to play with the words, not the concepts. Shakespeare is somehow more objective: there is less of his own viewpoint in his plays, rather a world awareness.

Jonson's plays, and *The Fair Maid of the West* and *The Rover* involved a great deal of physical movement which sometimes made speaking the lines to the whole house technically difficult. And though the movement obviously helped to release the language, it was difficult to make it your own without it being somehow self-conscious, somehow to do with 'I am being big and generous and taking you all in'. The balance was difficult to find – to find the joy of the movement and of the language as springing from the same thing.

When the plays transferred from the Swan to the Mermaid it was necessary to do fresh work on the voice, although time was limited. The Mermaid is not so easy to pitch to as the Swan – the audiences are further away, and it takes more conscious effort, though ideally of course this should not show. Now we will be taking the shows into The Pit, the adjustment should be a lot easier. I was surprised at how well *The Jew of Malta* transferred to the main Barbican stage – it was great, and seemed to open it out extraordinarily well. That house is difficult to play as it is so wide, and so voices can get unfocused very easily.

The set for *Hyde Park* was helpful in that it gave the actors natural places as focal points; and Fiona Shaw judged the language and the wit exactly right. Similarly, the set for *The New Inn* which built a stage on a stage, was easy to focus on. Such sets help the actors to find their strong points on that large promontory stage. A number of productions discovered the strength of the space above the stage, roughly level with the first gallery. Any theatre has problems of blocking, of points where the voice gets lost, or difficult places to reach. Antony Sher has commented on the unnatural posture one has to adopt to look at the audience in the top gallery, and to project to them. It has to be larger than life – and so all sorts of balances between reality and presentation come into question and have to be resolved.

I think we have used the Swan so far to rather similar effect, more perhaps to do with entertainment than to do with challenging an audience. Perhaps we need to be more adventurous in developing its potential. There is a tendency to get the audience involved in a friendly way only, and there are therefore dangers of becoming too jokey, too extravagant. Here it is so much different from the Main House.

The Swan space is certainly friendly and not at all threatening. Even a savage play like *Titus Andronicus* seemed perhaps more full of pathos than of cruelty. And this quality perhaps does not provoke the audience to question. I do think this is to do with the nature of the space, and we still have to learn more about it. It is going to be interesting to do modern plays here.

The extent to which I work on language in the Company depends very much on the time available, and on the individual directors. Work is done all the time on breathing, relaxation, and muscularity — that is how actors keep prepared. However, some directors see the work simply as a way to facilitate actors and to help them, others see it in more basic terms as helping to release the inner energy of the play. We are there to do both. If the actor is really living in and through the imagery the language will develop naturally. For instance, the tension and corruption within the *The Revenger's Tragedy* is rooted in the clotted images. The danger of the court is expressed in that language and in the movement of the dance, which became literally a dance for one's life. I did a lot of work at the beginning of rehearsals with Antony Sher to help release this language movement — it was a very difficult part, but wonderfully done. Through the language he conveyed all the tension and corruption of that world. You felt that language was the only way of expressing himself.

The language of Barabas in *The Jew of Malta*, as spoken by Alun Armstrong, was that of someone totally at ease with his world — however grotesque the events. Alun has a great gift of making the language seem like his own, however extravagant and improbable it is. He gets a connection with the language and an ease with it which makes it sound almost modern. Barabas has a very special kind of black humour which Alun found — he has great warmth as an actor.

There are conflicting views of *The New Inn*. This may be because the whole play is based on the play-acting of a game, and the characters themselves are not easy to grasp; they seem to have little complexity. The play needs great lightness of touch, with the emphasis on role-playing, and I think it was difficult to find its reality and substance. However, I found Lovel's long speeches quite surprising. They seemed to come out of the play, and there was a sense of Jonson himself writing his own feelings and thoughts. There seemed to be something very personal coming right through from Jonson which was very moving — something I did not expect. And John Carlisle spoke these speeches beautifully; he has an extraordinarily rich and evocative voice. His Machevil at the beginning of *The Jew of Malta* was quite breathtaking. Sue Blane's designs for *The New Inn* I thought used the space wonderfully, and made it good for the actors to work in.

To conclude, I think that the space is a challenge to actors to find the sense of reality in the writing, and yet to be able to convey that to all the areas of the theatre without coarsening or devaluing the language in any way. This is quite a task.

Door handles for the main entrance to the Swan
from the garden, designed by Antony Robinson.
PHOTOGRAPH: NICHOLAS SARGEANT

Madrigal sung by the entire cast at the conclusion of Ben Jonson's *Every Man in His Humour*.

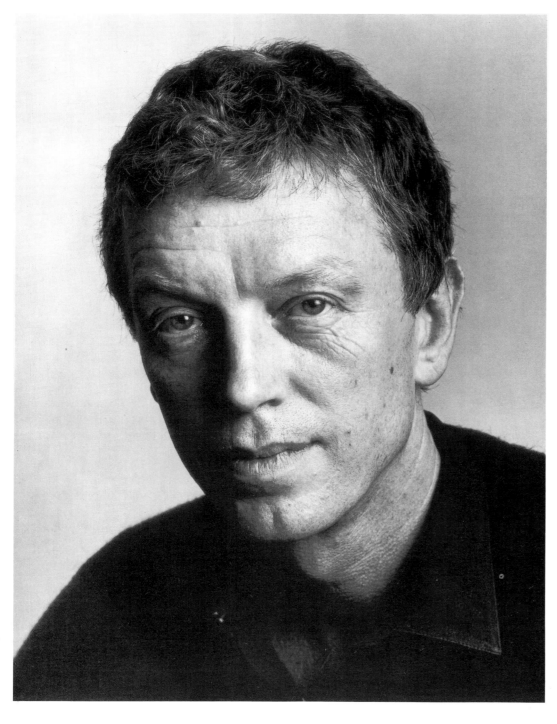

Terry Hands *studied at Birmingham University and R.A.D.A. In 1964 he was one of the founders of the Liverpool Everyman Theatre. He joined the RSC in 1966 and became Artistic Director of the RSC's Theatre-go-round from 1966–68. He has directed over forty productions of plays and operas, nationally and internationally. His productions for the RSC have included all four plays in the centenary season at Stratford in 1975, the three parts of* Henry VI, Coriolanus, As You Like It, Richard II *and* Richard III. *By 1980 he had directed the complete cycle of Shakespeare's history plays for the RSC, with Alan Howard in the leading roles. From 1975–78 he was Consultant Director for the Comédie Française, and in 1975 was appointed Chevalier of Arts and Letters by the French Government. In 1978 he became joint Artistic Director of the RSC and from 1986 has been Artistic Director and Chief Executive. His most recent productions for the RSC have included Peter Barnes's* Red Noses, Othello, The Winter's Tale, Julius Caesar, *Genet's* The Balcony *and* Carrie. *He is scheduled to direct* Romeo and Juliet *in the Swan in 1989.*

Towards the Future

TERRY HANDS

I remember standing with Trevor and John Barton in John's fifteenth-century dovecote at Hillborough looking up at the walls. Inside it is like a brick collander with each hole a dove's nest. 'That's how it should be', said someone, 'The walls papered with people'. The phrase stuck and, thanks to Michael Reardon's loving craft, so did the inspiration. He created a theatre at once old and new. Perhaps the first survivor of the time-lag between concept (70's) and execution (80's), unusually it was not already obsolete by the time it opened. The Swan is timeless.

The Main House at Stratford is a designer's theatre. It demands a pictorial context. Even with the extended forestage which gives it a unique hybrid quality – combining 'reality' with 'illusion' – it remains as much visual as verbal. The layout and indeed proportion of audience to stage accentuates the feeling of cinema. Like any proscenium theatre what you see is as important as what you hear. Not so the Swan. It resists design signature. Illusion doesn't work, nor a dependence upon sophisticated theatre vocabulary. The actor is dominant and what he says, feels, thinks is magnified by his centrality. Consequently only what is immediate to him has currency – costume for instance, props. Context must be carried by his performance, not his surroundings. The Swan is truly a place for people not things, and the audience is its architecture.

The Other Place – like The Pit – is a voyeuristic space. The audience is an intruder invited to peer in upon a ritual which has its own independent life. *Revenger's Tragedy* sat better in The Pit, so too did *Titus*. Surprisingly, The Other Place responds well to scenery, particularly for modern plays, but the acting is at its best when like television it ignores the audience. In the Swan the public is too powerful, too present to be ignored. It demands participation. The actors can do anything except for one minute forget that they are actors performing to and for an audience. It is this realism, this honesty, which makes the Swan such a thrilling theatre. You can't just talk to the air in the Swan, it is full of people; nor *at* the audience, it must be *to* them. At every turn there are faces and their concentration is invasive. Which makes it a perfect house for Shakespeare.

We have tried two Shakespeares so far and there are more to come. All the comedies should work there, and the lighter tragedies like *Romeo* and *Othello*, as well as the 'concertos' *Hamlet*, *Richard II*, *Richard III*. The Swan feels like Shakespeare's own theatre might have been – seemingly both open-air and enclosed – the simplest debating platform, a space for the imagination. Equally it suits his contemporaries Marlowe, Jonson, Tourneur – though Tourneur's claustrophobia is harder to achieve than the others' exuberance. Indeed if there is any danger with the Swan it is of a generalised warmhearted bonhomie – such is the extraordinary atmosphere that good nature and good will can produce. We have yet to succeed entirely with tragedy. The Restoration writers we must try again. Had the plays been more inhabited, and less commented upon, they might have been more successful. Certainly the ideas are there, and the language, but the productions showed that context must come from people – how they behave and why – not from externals. The writers themselves are already commenting; it is dangerous to comment further.

We have learned a lot in three years. More don'ts than do's, as always. Don't break the geometry of the Swan itself, don't pretend, don't take for granted, don't hide. And there have been some 'do's': *Every Man*, *The Fair Maid*, *The New Inn*.

So what of the future? Provided the play depends upon its language, debate, the direct confrontation of actor and audience, then I can see few limits. Molière and Marivaux should be naturals. Some of the nineteenth-century authors: plays like *An Enemy of the People*, for instance, perhaps *The Seagull*, certainly *Peer Gynt*. All the Greeks. But if it is to have real validity, the Swan must become a new-play house as well. We have started looking and indeed commissioning, but most new writing is either proscenium-orientated or small-space. To fit the Swan, new writing needs an awareness of the public arena not just a private vision. It needs a recoining of language, not just an acceptance. It needs universal themes rather than minority interests – questions not answers – theatricality in a proper sense. Above all, it needs complicity with the audience. Edward Bond's *Restoration* has pointed the way. The Swan remains both opportunity and challenge.

It is still early days. We need a further ten years of experiment, of success and failure, of intent and accident, and then I suspect the Swan will lead the RSC more surely into the twenty-first century than any of its other auditoria.

London,
January 1989

Appendix I

Between Script and Stage: Trevor Nunn's 'Pre-Show' and 'Induction Scene' for Heywood's *The Fair Maid of the West*

One of the most exciting aspects of Trevor Nunn's boisterous conflation of Thomas Heywood's plays called *The Fair Maid of the West* was the natural integration of the stage and auditorium into the world of an Elizabethan Tavern. Solid trestle tables and benches formed most of the stage furniture, furniture that could be adapted, upturned or draped to serve as a whole variety of improvised locations from a great ship to the court of the colourful King of Fez. The barmaid, and drinkers, decide to put on their own play, improvising parts and costumes in an unlikely celebration of the beautiful Bess Bridges and her adventures. The stage, and indeed much of the auditorium, was full of continuous action from the moment that the landlord, in the specially-written 'Pre-Show' welcomed the audience/guests, offering wine and good cheer. The arrival of the players, with a bombastic prologue in the vein of the Player King, but echoing the words of the Chorus from *Henry V*, is greeted with derision in the inn. The revellers have their own play in mind. Trevor Nunn's Induction scene owed something to the RSC's production of Beaumont's *The Knight of the Burning Pestle* as well as to a whole variety of famous Elizabethan and Jacobean prologues and choruses. And as the good natured chaos subsides, the visiting players, along with the tavern 'regulars', unite to set the scene for the audience with 'The Story of Bess Bridges'. The self-appointed book-keeper explains:

> Far from the courts of mighty Emperors
> Far from the deeds we understand from books
> To tavern, room and shipboard must we now
> Transport the setting of our travelling stage.

Trevor Nunn has been generous enough to allow us to print this newly devised sequence, along with the various blocking, setting and lighting details, direct from the prompt copy of his production, now held in the Company's Archive at the Shakespeare Centre. It offers a rare opportunity to see a process at work, leading towards the polished, if apparently improvised, opening of a play scarcely known now except in the study, but exceedingly popular in its own day. The record of that process includes the names of the current company, interspersed with some characters, and with all the directions and cues for actions and sounds meticulously noted. Even so, the words and pencil markings on the page can only record one person's observations of one moment in a rehearsal schedule. No performance is ever fixed. And, above all, no performance lives without its full visual and aural dimensions.

Trevor Nunn talks elsewhere of the importance of casting, and about his long wish to stage this particular show. Joe Melia and Simon Russell Beale recall their contributions to it, and our photographs attempt to evoke the atmosphere. But no book can capture the breathtaking skill of the fights, directed by Malcolm Ranson, or the folk-song quality of the music of Shaun Davey, or the audience's sheer delight at the pantomime world evoked by the court of Fez.

As Michael Billington wrote for *The Guardian* (24 September 1986):

We are not dealing here . . . with an imperishable masterpiece but with an exotic piece of pop-theatre about female fidelity, gang-loyalty and English adventuring. Heywood was a master-hack but the key-word in his two plays is 'ecstasy'; and Nunn seizes on that to give us an ecstatic form of rough theatre in which the emphasis is on narrative speed, and

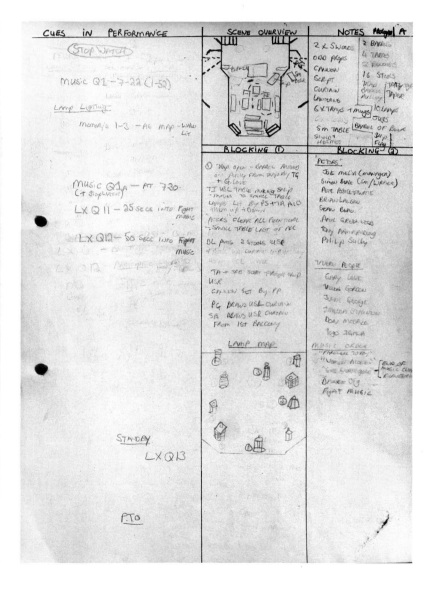

transformation of simple props, through imaginative belief and the use of music to heighten emotion rather than as aural wallpaper.

[. . .] But why the production works is that it uses a good deal of sophistication to create simple-seeming effects. When Bess takes to the sea, for instance, John Napier's design suddenly transforms the whole Swan stage into a ship: ropes are tethered to the rail running round the stage, a couple of canvas sheets become two sails, benches and trestle-tables are arranged in step-formation to suggest multi-levelled decks.

It is infinitely more exciting than multi-million pound hi-tech design because it involves the spectator in an act of imaginative participation; and, when Bess's ship grapples with a Spanish galleon, a handful of muskets fired into the Swan

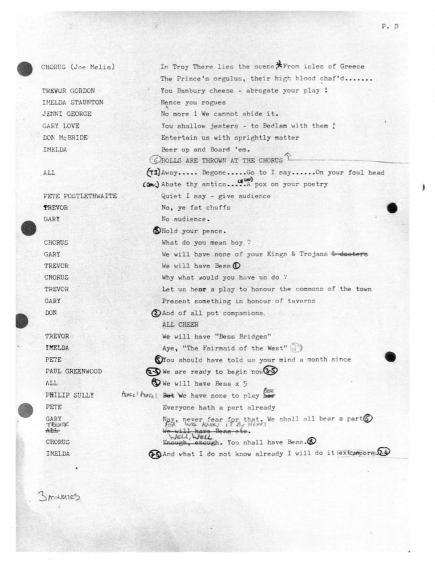

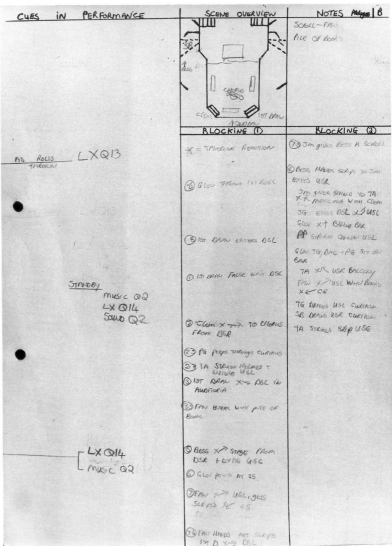

galleries and one actor swinging across the stage on a rope instantly convinces us we are in the midst of a sea-battle.

'In the midst' we certainly were. As the sketch from the prompt book (opposite the 'Pre-Show' speech) shows, Trevor Nunn and John Napier made use of steps down to the audience at the two front corners of the stage although the whole 'tongue' was surrounded by a low balustrade over which

actors stepped and on which they sat and stood. These features, combined with blocks, tables, and benches, gave a whole variety of possible levels for performers to use, constantly varying the picture and filling the space with activity. Indeed the whole piece emerged 'as a rip-roaring piece of popular entertainment suggesting Dick Whittington and Raiders of the Lost Ark have gone into partnership' (Michael Billington, *The Guardian*, 24 September 1986).

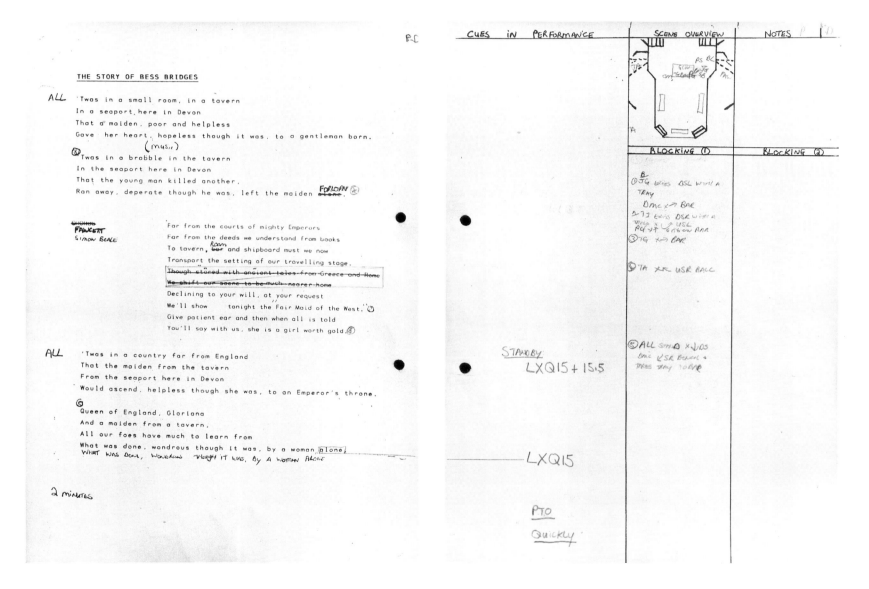

Appendix II

Cast Lists and Production Credits

The cast lists (and productions credits) are reproduced, by permission, from the *Swan Theatre Plays* series published by Methuen by arrangement with the RSC. The lists give the original casts for each play, which may have changed on transfer to London or Newcastle or for other reasons.

THE TWO NOBLE KINSMEN	*by William Shakespeare and John Fletcher*
EVERY MAN IN HIS HUMOUR	*by Ben Jonson*
THE ROVER	*by Aphra Behn*
THE FAIR MAID OF THE WEST	*by Thomas Heywood*
HYDE PARK	*by James Shirley*
TITUS ANDRONICUS	*by William Shakespeare*
THE JEW OF MALTA	*by Christopher Marlowe*
THE REVENGER'S TRAGEDY	*by Cyril Tourneur*
THE NEW INN	*by Ben Jonson*
THE CONSTANT COUPLE	*by George Farquhar*
THE PLAIN DEALER	*by William Wycherley*
THE MAN OF MODE	*by George Etherege*
RESTORATION	*by Edward Bond*

Swan Theatre

CAST

for the first public performance of this
RSC production on 26 April 1986.

Theseus *Duke of Athens*	**Peter Guinness**
Hippolyta *Queen of the Amazons*	**Anna Nygh**
Emilia *her sister*	**Amanda Harris**
Pirithous *friend of Theseus*	**Robert Morgan**
First Queen ⎫ *widows of Kings*	**Rosalind Boxall**
Second Queen ⎬ *killed in the*	**Jenni George**
Third Queen ⎭ *Siege of Thebes*	**Lucy Hancock**
Artesius *an Athenian soldier*	**Philip Sully**
Palamon ⎫ *the two*	**Gerard Murphy**
Arcite ⎬ *noble kinsmen*	**Hugh Quarshie**
Valerius *a Theban*	**John Patrick**
The Gaoler *of Theseus' prison*	**Robert Demeger**
Gaoler's Daughter	**Imogen Stubbs**
The Wooer *of Gaoler's Daughter*	**Donald McBride**
First Countryman	**Max Gold**
Second Countryman	**John Patrick**
Third Countryman	**Philip Sully**
Gerrold *a schoolmaster, in charge of the Morris*	**Richard Moore**
Countrywomen	**Rosalind Boxall**
	Jenni George
	Lucy Hancock
A Doctor	**Richard Moore**
Brother of Gaoler	**Max Gold**
Friends of Gaoler	**John Patrick**
	Philip Sully
Hymen/The Bavian/ The Messenger/The Executioner	**Joseph Mydell**
Boys	**James Lowrey**
	Robert Willey

Other parts played by members of the company

MUSICIANS

flute/alto flute/piccolo	**Ian Reynolds**
bassoon/keyboard	**Roger Hellyer**
horn	**Peter Morris**
horn	**David Statham**
percussion	**Nigel Garvey**
harp	**Brynmor Williams/ Audrey Douglas**

Directed by	**Barry Kyle**
Designed by	**Bob Crowley**
Movement by	**Ben Benison**
Music by	**Guy Woolfenden**
Lighting by	**Wayne Dowdeswell**
Company voice work by	**RSC Voice Department**
Music Director	**Roger Hellyer**
Sound by	**Mo Weinstock**
Design Assistant	**Jill Jowett**
Stage Manager	**Richard Oriel**
Deputy Stage Manager	**Chantal Hauser**
Assistant Stage Manager	**Jan Bevis Hughes/ Sarah Myatt**

This performance is approximately 3 hours long
including one interval of 20 minutes.

**Please do not smoke or use cameras or tape recorders
in the auditorium. And please remember that noise
such as whispering, coughing, rustling programmes
and the bleeping of digital watches can be distracting
to performers and also spoils the performance
for other members of the audience.**

Arts Council Funded

THE TWO NOBLE KINSMEN   *by William Shakespeare and John Fletcher*

Swan Theatre

CAST IN ORDER OF APPEARANCE

Old Kno'well	**Tony Church**
Brainworm, *his servant*	**David Haig**
Master Stephen, *his nephew*	**Paul Greenwood**
Servant	**Roger Moss**
Ed Kno'well, *Old Kno'well's son*	**Simon Russell Beale**
Master Matthew	**Philip Franks**
Cob	**David Troughton**
Tib, *his wife*	**Susie Fairfax**
Captain Bobadill	**Pete Postlethwaite**
Thomas Kitely	**Henry Goodman**
Thomas Cash, *his clerk*	**Gary Love**
George Downright, *brother to Wellbred*	**Jeremy Pearce**
Dame Kitely	**Jane Galloway**
Bridget, *Kitely's sister*	**Joely Richardson**
Wellbred, *brother to Downright*	**Nathaniel Parker**
Justice Clement	**Raymond Bowers**
Roger Formal, *his clerk*	**Mark Lindley**
Clement's servant	**Roger Moss**

Directed by	**John Caird**
Designed by	**Sue Blane**
Lighting by	**Wayne Dowdeswell**
Sound by	**John Leonard/ Mo Weinstock**
Fights by	**Malcolm Ranson**
Company voice work by	**Cicely Berry** and **David Carey**
Music Director	**Guy Woolfenden**
Design Assistant	**Jill Jowett**
Stage Manager	**Richard Oriel**
Deputy Stage Manager	**Jondon Gourkan/ Chantal Hauser**
Assistant Stage Manager	**Sarah Myatt/ Jan Bevis Hughes**

This performance is approximately 3 hours long including one interval of 20 minutes.

First performance of this RSC production, Swan Theatre, Stratford-upon-Avon, 15 May 1986

Please do not smoke or use cameras or tape recorders in the auditorium. And please remember that noise such as whispering, coughing, rustling programmes and the bleeping of digital watches can be distracting to performers and also spoils the performance for other members of the audience.

Arts Council Funded

EVERY MAN IN HIS HUMOUR   *by Ben Jonson*

Swan Theatre

CAST IN ORDER OF APPEARANCE

Belvile, *a Colonel*   **Hugh Quarshie**
Frederick, *his friend*   *four come out*   **Peter Guinness**
Blunt, *a country gull*   *of England*   **David Troughton**
Willmore, *the Rover*   **Jeremy Irons**
Lucetta, *a whore*   **Caroline Johnson**
Sancho, *her man*   **Tony Armatrading**
Florinda   **Geraldine Fitzgerald**
Valeria   *three sisters*   **Lucy Hancock**
Hellena   **Imogen Stubbs**
Don Pedro, *their brother*   **Nathaniel Parker**
Stephano   **Trevor Gordon**
Callis   *his servants*   **Jenni George**
Angellica Bianca, *a famous courtesan*   **Sinead Cusack**
Moretta, *her woman*   **Rosalind Boxall**
Sebastian   **Togo Igawa**
Biskey   *her bravos*   **Patrick Robinson**
Don Antonio, *the Viceroy's son*   **Philip Sully**
Diego, *his servant*   **Stan Pretty**
Phillip, *servant to the English*   **Brian Lawson**
Masquers/servants   **Tony Armatrading**
   Jenni George
   Trevor Gordon
   Togo Igawa
   Caroline Johnson
   Brian Lawson
   Stan Pretty
   Patrick Robinson

Directed by   **John Barton**
Designed by   **Louise Belson**
Lighting by   **Wayne Dowdeswell**
Music by   **Guy Woolfenden**
Company voice work by   **Cicely Berry** and **David Carey**

Design Assistant   **Jill Jowett**
Stage Manager   **Michael Dembowicz**
Deputy Stage Manager   **Graham Watts**
Assistant Stage Manager   **Matthew Purves**

This performance is approximately 2 hours 45 minutes long including one interval of 20 minutes.

First performance of this RSC production, Swan Theatre, Stratford-upon-Avon, 3 July 1986

Please do not smoke or use cameras or tape recorders in the auditorium. And please remember that noise such as whispering, coughing, rustling programmes and the bleeping of digital watches can be distracting to performers and also spoils the performance for other members of the audience.

Arts Council Funded

THE ROVER   *by Aphra Behn*

RSC
Swan Theatre

COMPANY IN ALPHABETICAL ORDER		MUSICIANS	
Tony Armatrading	Bashaw Joffer/Second Captain	flute	Ian Reynolds
Simon Russell Beale	Fawcett	oboe/keyboard	John Woolf
Sean Bean	Spencer	bassoon	Roger Hellyer
Jenni George	Queen Tota	violin	Richard Springate
Trevor Gordon	Drawer/Sailor/Spanish Prisoner	violoncello	Alan Carus-Wilson
Paul Greenwood	Captain Goodlack	guitar	John Richards
Togo Igawa	Bashaw Alcade	harp	Audrey Douglas
Brian Lawson	First Captain/Alderman/	uileann pipes/trumpet	Robert White
	Spanish Captain	percussion	Nigel Garvey
Gary Love	Drawer/Sailor/Spanish Prisoner		
Donald McBride	Clem		
Joe Melia	Mayor/King Mullisheg		
Pete Postlethwaite	Roughman	Directed by	Trevor Nunn
Imelda Staunton	Bess Bridges	Set designed by	John Napier
Philip Sully	Carrol/Singer/Surgeon/	Costumes designed by	Andreane Neofitou
	Bandit Chief/Merchant	Lighting by	Wayne Dowdeswell
		Music by	Shaun Davey
		Fights by	Malcolm Ranson

The many other parts are played by the company

Company voice work by **Cicely Berry** and **David Carey**

This production is sponsored by

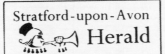

Stratford-upon-Avon Herald

Music Director	John Woolf
Assistant Director	Jude Kelly
Stage Manager	Rachael Whitteridge
Deputy Stage Manager	Graham Watts
Assistant Stage Manager	Debra Hardy

This performance is approximately 3 hours long, including one interval of 20 minutes.

First performance of this RSC production: Swan Theatre, Stratford-upon-Avon, 11 September 1986.

Please do not smoke or use cameras or tape recorders in the auditorium. And please remember that noise such as whispering, coughing, rustling programmes and the bleeping of digital watches can be distracting to performers and also spoils the performance for other members of the audience.

Arts Council Funded

THE FAIR MAID OF THE WEST   *by Thomas Heywood*

Swan Theatre

CAST IN ORDER OF APPEARANCE		MUSICIANS	
Trier	James Fleet	piano	John Woolf
Lacy	Richard McCabe	flute	Ian Reynolds
Venture	Paul Spence	clarinet	Edward Watson
Jarvis	Bill McGuirk	trumpet/cornet	Brian Allen
Lord Bonvile	John Carlisle	cello	Alan Carus-Wilson
Lord Bonvile's Page	David Pullan	percussion	Clifford Pick
Rider	Sean Pertwee		
Mistress Bonavent	Pippa Guard	Directed by	Barry Kyle
Mistress Carol	Fiona Shaw	Designed by	Gerard Howland
Fairfield	Alex Jennings	Lighting by	Wayne Dowdeswell
Master Bonavent	Paul Webster	Music by	Jeremy Sams
Julietta	Felicity Dean	Movement by	Sheila Falconer
A Waiting Woman	Kate Littlewood	Sound by	Paul Slocombe
Jockey	Laban Leake	Music Director	John Woolf
Stable Lad	Jeremy Gilley	Assistant Director	Nicholas Mahon
Milkmaid	Jane Whittenshaw	Company voice work by	RSC Voice Department
Wedding Guests	Kate Littlewood	Stage Manager	Rachael Whitteridge
	Jane Whittenshaw	Deputy Stage Manager	Alastair John-Duncan
	Jeremy Gilley	Assistant Stage Manager	Susan Dale
	Laban Leake		
Runners	Jeremy Gilley		
	Laban Leake		

Other parts are played by members of the company.

'At the age of eight the young Virginia Woolf edited her first publication, a newspaper for family and friends. It was called the "Hyde Park Gate News".'

First performance of this RSC production: Swan Theatre, Stratford-upon-Avon, 7 April 1987.

Arts Council Funded

HYDE PARK   *by James Shirley*

Swan Theatre

CAST

ROMANS		GOTHS	
Saturninus, *son to the late Emperor of Rome and afterwards Emperor*	**Jim Hooper**	Tamora, *Queen of the Goths*	**Estelle Kohler**
Bassianus, *brother to Saturninus*	**Mike Dowling**	Alarbus	**Steven Elliott**
Titus Andronicus, *a noble Roman, general against the Goths*	**Brian Cox**	Demetrius *sons to Tamora*	**Piers Ibbotson**
		Chiron	**Richard McCabe**
Marcus Andronicus, *tribune of the People, and brother to Titus*	**Donald Sumpter**	Aaron, a Moor, *beloved by Tamora*	**Peter Polycarpou**
		1st Goth Soldier	**Mike Dowling**
Lucius	**Derek Hutchinson**	2nd Goth Soldier	**Steven Elliott**
Quintus *sons to Titus Andronicus*	**Ian Bailey**	3rd Goth Soldier	**Linus Roache**
Martius	**Linus Roache**		
Mutius	**Sean Pertwee**	Directed by	**Deborah Warner**
Lavinia, *daughter to Titus Andronicus*	**Sonia Ritter**	Designed by	**Isabella Bywater**
Young Lucius, *a boy, son to Lucius*	**Jeremy Gilley**	Lighting by	**Wayne Dowdeswell**
Publius, *son to Marcus Andronicus*	**Sean Pertwee**	Company voice work by	**RSC Voice Department**
Sepronius	**Steven Elliott**	Assistant Director	**Bill Buffery**
Caius *Kinsmen to Titus*	**Linus Roache**	Stage Manager	**Rachael Whitteridge**
Valentine	**Ian Bailey**	Deputy Stage Manager	**Maralyn Sarrington**
Aemilius, *a noble Roman*	**Dennis Clinton**	Assistant Stage Manager	**Anne Rushworth**
Messenger	**Steven Elliott**		
Nurse	**Jane Whittenshaw**		
Clown	**Mike Dowling**		

First performance of this RSC production: Swan Theatre, Stratford-upon-Avon, 28 April 1987

Please do not smoke or use cameras or tape recorders in the auditorium. And please remember that noise such as whispering, coughing, rustling programmes and the bleeping of digital watches can be distracting to performers and also spoils the performance for other members of the audience.

Arts Council Funded

TITUS ANDRONICUS

by William Shakespeare

Swan Theatre

CAST

Machevil — **John Carlisle**

THE JEWS

Barabas — **Alun Armstrong**
Abigail, *his daughter* — **Janet Amsbury**
First Jew — **Michael Cadman**
Second Jew — **George Raistrick**
Third Jew — **Geoffrey Freshwater**

THE KNIGHTS AND PEOPLE OF MALTA

Ferneze, *the Governor* — **John Carlisle**
Lodowick, *his son* — **James Fleet**
First Knight of Malta — **Bill McGuirk**
Knight Officer — **Dennis Clinton**
Knight Officer — **Ian Bailey**
Knight Officer — **Richard Leaf**
Katherine, *a Gentlewoman* — **Linda Spurrier**
Don Mathias, *her son* — **Gregory Doran**
Bellamira, *a courtesan* — **Stella Gonet**
Pilia-Borza, *a thief* — **Barrie Rutter**
First Merchant Seaman — **Ian Bailey**
Second Merchant Seaman — **Dennis Clinton**

THE FRIARS AND NUNS

Friar Jacomo — **Geoffrey Freshwater**
Friar Bernardine — **George Raistrick**
Abbess — **Shirley King**
A Nun — **Deborah Goodman**

THE TURKS

Selim-Calymath — **Peter Polycarpou**
Callapine — **Akim Mogaji**
Bashaw — **Gregory Doran**

THE SPANISH

Martin del Bosco,
Vice-Admiral of Spain — **Michael Cadman**

SLAVES

Ithamore — **Phil Daniels**
Turkish Slave — **Richard Leaf**
Moorish Slave — **Akim Mogaji**
Slave Girl — **Deborah Goodman**

MUSICIANS

flute — **Ian Reynolds**
clarinet — **Edward Watson**
trumpet — **Robert Pritchard**
trumpet — **Peter Fisher**
trombone — **Gareth Richards**
percussion — **Nigel Garvey/James Jones**
keyboard — **John Woolf/**
Michael Tubbs

Directed by — **Barry Kyle**
Designed by — **Bob Crowley**
Lighting by — **Wayne Dowdeswell**
Music by — **Ilona Sekacz**
Fights by — **Malcolm Ranson**
Sound by — **Mc Weinstock**
Dialect Coach — **Joan Washington**
Music Director — **Michael Tubbs/**
John Woolf
Assistant Director — **Nicholas Mahon**
Stage Manager — **Charles Evans**
Deputy Stage Manager — **Eric Lumsden**
Assistant Stage Manager — **Martyn Sergent**

Sponsored by

Herald Press

First performance of this RSC production: Swan Theatre, Stratford-upon-Avon, 7 July 1987.
Please do not smoke or use cameras or tape recorders in the auditorium. And please remember that noise such as whispering, coughing, rustling programmes and the bleeping of digital watches can be distracting to performers and also spoils the performance for other members of the audience.

Arts Council Funded

THE JEW OF MALTA   *by Christopher Marlowe*

Swan Theatre

CAST

Vindice	**Antony Sher**
Hippolito, *Vindice's brother*	**Sean Baker**
Gratiana, *Vindice's mother*	**Linda Spurrier**
Castiza, *Vindice's sister*	**Stella Gonet**
Dondola, *servant to Gratiana*	**Michael Loughnan**
The Duke	**David Howey**
The Duchess	**Julie Legrand**
Supervacuo, *the Duchess's second son*	**Mike Dowling**
Ambitioso, *the Duchess's eldest son*	**Jim Hooper**
Lussurioso, *the Duke's son by a previous marriage, and his heir*	**Nicholas Farrell**
Spurio, *the Duke's bastard son*	**Phil Daniels**
Junior, *the Duchess's youngest son*	**Steven Elliott**
Antonio } *noblemen attending at the*	**Ian Barritt**
Piero } *Duke's court*	**Richard Leaf**
Nencio }	**Ian Bailey**
Sordido } *followers of Lussurioso*	**Patrick Cremin**
First Judge	**Patrick Cremin**
Second Judge	**Ian Bailey**
Attendants	**Henrietta Bess**
	Susan Harper-Browne

Directed by	**Di Trevis**
Designed by	**Michael Levine**
Movement Director	**Jane Gibson**
Lighting by	**Gerry Jenkinson and Ben Ormerod**
Music by	**Dominic Muldowney**
Sound by	**Dominic Muldowney and Mo Weinstock**
Company Voice Work by	**RSC Voice Department**
Assistant Director	**Nicholas Mahon**
Stage Manager	**Charles Evans**
Deputy Stage Manager	**Eric Lumsden**
Assistant Stage Manager	**Cas Fail**

First performace of this RSC production: Swan Theatre, Stratford-upon-Avon, 2 September 1987.

Please do not smoke or use cameras or tape recorders in the auditorium. And please remember that noise such as whispering, coughing, rustling programmes and the bleeping of digital watches can be distracting to performers and also spoils the performance for other members of the audience.

THE REVENGER'S TRAGEDY   *by Cyril Tourneur*

CAST IN ORDER OF APPEARANCE

Goodstock, *The Host*	**Joseph O'Conor**
Ferret	**Peter Polycarpou**
Lovel	**John Carlisle**
Frank	**Sonia Ritter**
Prudence	**Deborah Findlay**
Lady Frampul	**Fiona Shaw**
Nurse	**Darlene Johnson**
Trundle	**Trevor Martin**
Beaufort	**Gregory Doran**
Latimer	**Mike Dowling**
Sir Glorious Tipto	**Richard McCabe**
Fly	**Clive Russell**
Pierce	**Sean Pertwee**
Jug	**Sally George**
Jordan	**Griffith Jones**
Peck	**Jimmy Gardner**
Bat Burst	**William Chubb**
Hodge Huffle	**Ian Bailey**
Barnaby	**Laban Leake**
Nick Stuff	**Ian Barritt**
Pinnacia Stuff	**Jane Leonard**

MUSICIANS

violin	**Richard Springate**
violin	**Gillian Springate**
percussion	**James Jones**

Directed by	**John Caird**
Designed by	**Sue Blane**
Lighting by	**Wayne Dowdeswell**
Music by	**Guy Woolfenden**
Assistant Director	**Bill Buffery**
Stage Manager	**Michael Dembowicz**
Deputy Stage Manager	**Alison Owen**
Assistant Stage Manager	**Jayne Hedley-Boreham**

Sponsored by
Royal Insurance

First performance of this RSC production: Swan Theatre, Stratford-upon-Avon, 4 November, 1987

Please do not smoke or use cameras or tape recorders in the auditorium. And please remember that noise such as whispering, coughing, rustling programmes and the bleeping of digital watches can be distracting to performers and also spoils the performance for other members of the audience.

Arts Council Funded

THE NEW INN   *by Ben Jonson*

CAST IN ORDER OF APPEARANCE

Footmen — **Stephen Jacobs**
Peter Lennon
James Purefoy
Ken Shorter
David Solomon
Melanie Thaw

Vizard — **David Acton**
outwardly pious, otherwise a great debauchee, and villainous

Alderman Smuggler — **Joe Melia**
an old Merchant

Colonel Standard — **Tony Armatrading**
a disbanded Colonel, brave and generous

Sir Harry Wildair — **Pip Donaghy**
an airy gentleman, affecting humorous gaiety and freedom in his behaviour

Clincher Senior — **Simon Russell Beale**
a pert London 'prentice turned Beau, and affecting travel

Lady Lurewell — **Maureen Beattie**
a Lady of a jilting temper, proceeding from a resentment of her wrongs from Men

Parly — **Jenni George**
Maid to Lady Lurewell

Clincher Junior — **Mark Sproston**
a Brother, educated in the Country

Dicky — **Stephen Jacobs**
his Man

Lady Darling — **Jill Spurrier**
an old Lady, Mother to Angelica

Angelica — **Amanda Root**
a Woman of Honour

Tom Errand — **Desmond Barrit**
a Porter

Tom Errand's Wife — **Claudette Williams**

Constable — **Ken Shorter**

Butler — **Peter Lennon**

Directed by — **Roger Michell**
Designed by — **Ultz**
Lighting by — **Wayne Dowdeswell**
Music by — **Jeremy Sams**
Choreography by — **Pat Garrett**
Music Director — **John Woolf**
Assistant Director — **Stephen Rayne**
Assistants to the Designer — **Nicky Gillibrand, Jeremy Herbert**
Company voice work by — **Cicely Berry** and **Andrew Wade**
Stage Manager — **Rachael Whitteridge**
Deputy Stage Manager — **Sheonagh Darby**
Assistant Stage Manager — **Philip Chard**

Understudies
Desmond Barrit Smuggler
Stephen Jacobs Clincher Junior
Peter Lennon Clincher Senior
James Purefoy Standard
Ken Shorter Tom Errand
David Solomon Vizard/Dicky
Mark Sproston Wildair
Jill Spurrier Tom Errand's Wife
Melanie Thaw Lady Lurewell/Angelica
Claudette Williams Lady Darling/Parly

Sponsored by

The performance is approximately 2½ hours in length, including one interval of fifteen minutes.

First performance of this production: Swan Theatre, Stratford-upon-Avon, 30 March 1988.

Please do not smoke or use cameras or tape recorders in the auditorium. And please remember that noise such as whispering, coughing, rustling programmes and the bleeping of digital watches can be distracting to performers and also spoils the performance for other members of the audience.

Arts Council Funded

THE CONSTANT COUPLE

by George Farquhar

Sponsored by
Royal Insurance

CAST IN ORDER OF APPEARANCE

Manly	**David Calder**
My Lord Plausible	**Tom Fahy**
First Sailor	**Trevor Gordon**
Second Sailor	**Kevin Doyle**
Freeman	**Oliver Cotton**
Fidelia	**Geraldine Alexander**
The Widow Blackacre	**Marjorie Yates**
Jerry Blackacre	**Jason Watkins**
Olivia	**Joanne Pearce**
Eliza	**Jaye Griffiths**
Lettice	**Cissy Collins**
Olivia's Boy	**Anthony Dixon**
Olivia's Maid	**Kathleen Christof**
Novel	**Mark Hadfield**
Major Oldfox	**Nicholas Smith**
Alderman	**Edward Peel**
Quaint	**Kathleen Christof**
Splitcause	**Cissy Collins**
Petulant	**Kevin Doyle**
Bookseller's Boy	**Anthony Dixon**
Vernish	**Edward Peel**
First Knight of the Post	**Kevin Doyle**
Second Knight of the Post	**Cissy Collins**
Waitress	**Kathleen Christof**
Waiter	**Anthony Dixon**
Bailiff	**Trevor Gordon**

Musicians

Harpsichord	**John Woolf**
Violins	**Richard Springate**
	Gillian Springate
'Cello	**Alan Carus-Wilson**

Music by	**Henry Purcell**
Arranged and adapted by	**Guy Woolfenden**

Directed by	**Ron Daniels**
Designed by	**David Fielding**
Movement Director	**Jane Gibson**
Lighting by	**Wayne Dowdeswell**
Fight Director	**Malcolm Ranson**
Music Director	**John Woolf**
Assistant Director	**Katie Mitchell**
Stage Manager	**Michael Dembowicz**
Deputy Stage Manager	**Ian Barber**
Assistant Stage Manager	**Sarah West Stevens**

First performance of this production: Swan Theatre, Stratford-upon-Avon, 20 April 1988.

Please do not smoke or use cameras or tape recorders in the auditorium. And please remember that noise such as whispering, coughing, rustling programmes and the bleeping of digital watches can be distracting to performers and also spoils the performance for other members of the audience.

Arts Council Funded

THE PLAIN DEALER   *by William Wycherley*

CAST

Mr Dorimant	**Miles Anderson**
Handy, *his valet*	**John Bott**
Foggy Nan, *an orange-woman*	**Jane Cox**
Mr Medley	**Pip Donaghy**
Shoemaker/Chairman/Footman	**David Acton**
Young Bellair	**Mark Sproston**
Lady Townley, *sister to Old Bellair*	**Joan Blackham**
Emilia	**Jenni George**
Old Bellair	**Joe Melia**
John Trott/Footman	**Edward Rawle-Hicks**
Mrs Loveit's Page/Footman	**David Solomon**
Mrs Loveit, *in love with Dorimant*	**Marie Mullen**
Pert	**Maureen Beattie**
Belinda *in love with Dorimant*	**Katy Behean**
Harriet	**Amanda Root**
Busy	**Claudette Williams**
Lady Woodvil	**Patricia Lawrence**
Sir Fopling Flutter	**Simon Russell Beale**
Smirk, *a Chaplain*/Chairman/Footman	**Timothy Stark**
Sir Fopling Flutter's Page	**Andrew Heron/ Joseph Steele**

Directed by	**Garry Hynes**
Designed by	**Ultz**
Lighting by	**Clive Morris**
Music by	**Ilona Sekacz**
Movement by	**Michael Popper**
Music Director	**Michael Tubbs**
Assistant Director	**Katie Mitchell**
Assistant to Ultz	**James Kronzer**
Stage Manager	**Jondon Gourkan**
Deputy Stage Manager	**Natasha Betteridge**
Assistant Stage Manager	**Kate Sarley**

Sponsored by
Royal Insurance

The performance is approximately 2¾ hours long, including one interval of 20 minutes.

First performance of this production: Swan Theatre, Stratford-upon-Avon, 6 July 1988.

Please do not smoke or use cameras or tape recorders. And please remember that noise such as whispering, coughing, rustling programmes and the bleeping of digital watches can be distracting to performers and also spoils the perfomance for other members of the audience.

Arts Council Funded

THE MAN OF MODE   *by George Etherege*

CAST IN ORDER OF APPEARANCE

Lord Are	**Simon Russell Beale**
Frank	**Mark Sproston**
Bob Hedges	**Duncan Bell**
Mr Hardache	**Colin McCormack**
Ann, Lady Are	**Melanie Thaw**
Rose	**Vivienne Rochester**
Mrs Hedges	**Pip Hinton**
Parson	**Joe Melia**
Gaoler	**John Bott**
Gabriel Hedges	**Alfred Burke**
Mrs Wilson	**Jane Cox**
Old Lady Are	**Patricia Lawrence**
Messenger	**Timothy Stark**

Directed by **Roger Michell**
Designed by **David Fielding**
Lighting by **Rick Fisher**
Music by **Ilona Sekacz**
Sound by **Paul Slocombe**
Dialect Coach **Joan Washington**
Company voice work by **Cicely Berry** and **Andrew Wade**
Music Director **John Woolf**
Assistant Director **Cordelia Monsey**
Stage Manager **Jondon Gourkan**
Deputy Stage Manager **Natasha Betteridge**
Assistant Stage Manager **Kate Sarley**

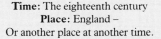
Sponsored by
Royal Insurance

Time: The eighteenth century
Place: England –
Or another place at another time.

PART ONE

Scene One	London: Lord Are's park
Scene Two	Hilgay: The Hall – Porch
Scene Three	Hilgay: The Hall – Lady Are's Drawing Room
Scene Four	Hilgay: The Hall – Workroom
Scene Five	Hilgay: The Hall – Breakfast Room

PART TWO

Scene One	Peterborough: Gaol – Cell
Scene Two	Hilgay: Copse
Scene Three	Peterborough: Holme Cottage – Kitchen
Scene Four	London: Old Lady Are's House – Drawing Room
Scene Five	Hilgay: The Hall – Breakfast Room
Scene Six	Peterborough: Holme Cottage – Kitchen
Scene Seven	London: London Bridge

First performance of this production: Swan Theatre, Stratford-upon-Avon, 7 September 1988.

The performance is approximately 2¾ hours long, including one interval of 20 minutes.

Please do not smoke or use cameras or tape recorders. And please remember that noise such as whispering, coughing, rustling programmes and the bleeping of digital watches can be distracting to performers and also spoils the performance for other members of the audience.

Arts Council Funded

RESTORATION

by Edward Bond

Acknowledgements

The enjoyment of working on this book has been much enhanced by the willing co-operation of a great many people. It has given us much pleasure to meet, and to learn from, each of those who have contributed to the book. We are indebted to all, within the RSC and outside it, who have given us written material, or whom we interviewed.

We are grateful, also, to a number of people who have helped us, but whose names do not appear elsewhere in this book. We have received wise counsel and generous help from David Brierley, General Manager of the RSC, Brian Glover, Curator of the RSC Collection, and Dr Levi Fox, Director of the Shakespeare Birthplace Trust and his staff, especially the Trust's Librarian, Mrs Marion Pringle.

Numerous further members of the RSC have been unstintingly and enthusiastically helpful to us. These include: Susan Davenport, Genista McIntosh, Mary Lee McNulty, Alison Holdom, Kate Jones, Emma Romer, Tamsin Thomas, Anne Tippett, Jenny Alden and Amanda Calvert.

It has been a great stimulus to bring this book together alongside the Exhibition mounted, under the same name, at the Mead Gallery, University of Warwick, during February and March, 1989. We are especially grateful to Katharine Eustace, Curator of the Mead Gallery and her staff, and to Helen Mallinson, who designed the Exhibition with flair and imagination. Many who assisted with the Exhibition should be thanked also, including Wayne Dowdeswell and Paul Slocumbe. Above all, Geoff Locker, of the RSC, whose contribution to the success of the Swan Theatre is beyond measure, has also contributed immeasurably to the enjoyment of our work for the Exhibition and for this book.

The University of Warwick made work on the book possible. The Research and Innovations sub-committee of the Estimates and Grants Committee gave us a generous grant that enabled us to begin. Students of the Graduate School of Renaissance Studies provided us with the results of their research on the Swan repertoire with skill and great good humour. We are indebted to: Catherine Charlton, Colleen Didur, Dawn Duddridge, José Gonzales, Nicholas Kneale, Julia Matthews, Joan McBrien, Glen Mynott, Tomoko Ohtani, Jennifer Parr, Ursula Ruston, Fenella Tookey, Muhammed Alyo, Jessica Gordon and Bob Godfrey. We are more than grateful, as always, to our secretaries, Janet Bailey and Brenda Doughty of the Graduate School, and Maureen Brown of Theatre Studies.

An exceptionally happy part of the experience of working on this book, written as it was to a very short deadline, has been the ready co-operation and skilled guidance of Mr Alec Jolly, Judith Boden-Cummins, Mr Mike Peake, Mr Tony Waugh and Mr Kevin Hines of Jolly & Barber Ltd, our printers. We are also immensely indebted, and not only financially, to Jaguar Cars Ltd, and especially to Mr John Maries of Jaguar.

Our chief debt we express in our dedication of the book to Eithne Mulryne and John Morris, for their patience and understanding as the demands of the book time and again played havoc with more domestic commitments.

RM., MS.